"A river is a liquid mountain, though yo[...] this way, until reading Walker's dram[...] venturing into the unknown. Like *In* [...] places from which there may be no return. [...] never paddled a stream will be that rivers are so alive, voice-filled, dangerous, and welcoming. Rivers are places, Walker writes, where the current 'flows but one direction — into the future.' Walker's experiences as an elite paddler, meditative and enormously dramatic, will have river veterans nodding in agreement and surprise. I loved the journey."

— **Doug Stanton, author of the #1 *New York Times* bestseller *Horse Soldiers***

"*Torrents As Yet Unknown* is an important contribution to the literature of exploration and the history of whitewater river running. But it is also a fascinating study of character — of the irrepressible imagination and sheer audacity of those who seek out the wildest places, who make a life of honing the skills needed to navigate the unknown at the extreme limit of human survivability. As I read, I found myself repeatedly murmuring, 'You can't make this stuff up.' From kayakers trying to maneuver on the Blue Nile while shooting attacking crocodiles with a pistol, to paddlers attempting to kayak from just below Everest's base camp, to Chinese scholars sealing themselves in closed capsules and asking to be shoved off into the ferocious cataclysm of the Yangtze River's Tiger Leaping Gorge. Walker knows the territory: he's a soldier and explorer who has led expeditions into Tibet's mythic Tsangpo Gorge, and singlehandedly paddled the first descents of many of Pakistan's whitewater rivers. His book had my pulse racing. And I kept thinking, 'That's why we love rivers, and that's why the greatest push the limits.'"

— **Peter Heller, author of *The Dog Stars, The River*, and *The Guide*.**

"It's not often that an all-time great explorer, paddling pioneer, and expedition leader writes an all-time great book on his life's obsession. But Wick Walker has done it, and it's a doozy. This compendium of whitewater first descents is a must-read for every adventure-lover — you don't need to be a kayaker or raft guide to feel the power of these stories."

— **Brian Castner, author of *Disappointment River: Finding and Losing the Northwest Passage***

"Superbly written and very, very gripping ... *Torrents As Yet Unknown* brought back to me rich memories, especially of Mike Jones, one of the great adventurers of our time."

— **Sir Chris Bonington, CVO, CBE, DL, mountaineer, and author of more than a dozen books about his adventures, including *Annapurna South Face***

Torrents As Yet Unknown

Torrents
As Yet
Unknown

*Daring
Whitewater Ventures
into the World's
Great River Gorges*

WICKLIFFE W. WALKER

STEER
FORTH
PRESS

LEBANON, NEW HAMPSHIRE

For information about permission to reproduce
selections from this book, write to:
Steerforth Press, 31 Hanover Street, Suite 1
Lebanon, New Hampshire 03766

Cataloging-in-Publication Data is available from the Library of Congress

Paperback ISBN 978-1-58642-390-2
Original Hardcover ISBN 978-1-58642-372-8

The frontispiece is a reproduction of an original
painting by artist Hoyt Reel, courtesy of Bob Gedekoh.

Maps by Molly O'Halloran

Illustrations by Kim Abney

Printed in the United States of America

To Tom McEwan:
explorer, teacher, and lifelong friend.

He prays to the genius of the place and to Earth, the first of the
gods, and to the Nymphs and as yet unknown rivers.
— Virgil (Publius Vergilius Maro), *Aeneid* 7.l.136

Contents

Preface

On every continent but Antarctica, rivers course through rugged mountain ranges and clefts in the terrain like arteries through Earth's body, gorges and canyons too inaccessible and hostile to serve as waterways for migration, trade, or conquest. These remain to this day places of spiritual wonder, of geographic enigma, of hidden danger and awesome beauty. The rivers don't carve only the bedrock; they shape the men and women who confront them as well, men and women frequently as relentless and complicated as the rivers they explore.

In the nineteenth century geographic exploration began to turn away from its utilitarian roots. Edward Whymper and the Duke of Abruzzi began reaching for the inhospitable mountain peaks of the Alps and the Americas; Robert Peary, Roald Amundsen, and Robert Falcon Scott for the frozen poles. Beneath a veneer of scientific curiosity lay an emerging foundation of romance and adventure. The profits sought were no longer gold, whales, or furs, nor the Northwest Passage to the Orient. These were journeys of pure discovery, for the science, for the adventure itself, for the books, for the packed lectures at the Royal Geographical Society and similar venues. And on May 24, 1869, when Major John Wesley Powell launched his four wooden dories down the Green River on his way to the Grand Canyon of the Colorado, a new discipline of whitewater expeditions joined these quests.

Yet while mountaineering evolved, developed its own traditions, and created a remarkable canon of climbing literature, for almost a century expedition whitewater remained stagnant. The dories remained of wood, the canoes of wood and canvas, the kayaks of sealskin or rubberized canvas stretched over a fragile skeleton. And the tumultuous mountain gorges remained beyond reach.

The second half of the twentieth century saw dramatic changes in the aftermath of World War II. War-spawned materials and industries, greater middle-class disposable income and leisure time in the West, and the proliferation of communist governments in the East all contributed to five decades of almost unbelievable growth in whitewater adventuring. Born in 1946 after my father's return from the Pacific Theater, I played a bit part in that whole process myself.

In the following chapters, I try to convey something of the wonder and awe of Earth's canyons and gorges, the thrill and adventure around each mysterious bend, and the remarkable pioneers who set new standards for river running.

It is not my intent to enumerate the "greatest" river gorges on the planet, nor the "most difficult" river expeditions, nor the "first descents" of any stretch of whitewater. Fools' errands, all. There is not even an agreed convention for determining the depth of a canyon. How wide from the river may the rims or bounding peaks be to count as measuring points? And why does it matter, except for bragging rights? Likewise, why compare running torrents measuring tens of thousands of cubic feet per second, like the Indus and Tsangpo Rivers, with steep, vertical-walled canyons with flows measured in the hundreds, like the Kali Gandaki and Colca Rivers?

The question of who, or which team, accomplished a first descent is usually equally immeasurable on these great gorges (Powell on the Grand Canyon being a notable exception). Different explorers often pick apart pieces of the puzzle, at different times and water levels, achieving different degrees of success, and opinions will vary about which is the true first descent.

Rather, I have selected river runs that I find of extraordinary interest because of their magnitude and diversity. Two are in North America, two in South America, one in Europe, two in Africa, and eight, appropriately, in the Himalayas or Tibetan Plateau. The explorers are equally diverse, from a nomadic group of Polish university students on a two-year odyssey, to a solo kayaker on an extreme three-day run, to a commercial rafting entrepreneur ringleading a television extravaganza. This diversification, however, leads also to omissions. I have left out many amazing canyons and extraordinary expeditions, some because I had too little access to the stories, some because I felt that I could add little to books and films already available. For example, I regret the absence from this volume of Walt Blackadar and Rob Lesser, two kayaking pioneers, both from Idaho, who were dominant figures in the 1970s and 1980s.

Powell published the popular account of his 1869 Grand Canyon descent more than two decades after the expedition. With a sense of broad perspective, he wrote: "Many years have passed since the exploration, and those who were boys with me in the enterprise are — ah, most of them are dead, and the living are gray with age." Most expedition accounts, however, have been produced shortly after return, when memories, emotions, and sometimes grief, were fresh. My purpose in this volume is to revisit these expeditions from a distance of time, through the lens of my own six decades of river experience and the reflections of the many explorers who have been generous in sharing with me their time, recollections, and records, including private diaries.

Finishing this narrative with an account of my own expedition to the Tsangpo in 1998 feels appropriate. It marked the first time that high-resolution satellite photography was available to the civilian world to reveal details about an inaccessible gorge in advance of going there, and satellite telephones had become small enough to carry in a kayak. As technology continues to advance and the Anthropocene flowers, some of the mystery and inaccessibility of the world's wild places is disappearing. Shrinking glaciers and other threats are degrading water sources and quality. Part of Major Powell's route down the Colorado has long since been consumed by the Glen Canyon Dam and Lake Powell, and ever bigger and more rapacious hydroelectric projects threaten gorges, including some of those featured in this book.

Some of Earth's most magical, perhaps even sacred, places become more endangered every year. We must appreciate them while we have them and record their wonders while we can.

"The current of the Green seems eager to bear us down through its mysterious canyons," wrote Major Powell. "We're just as eager to start, so off we go."

Wick Walker

Lexington, Virginia

January 2023

Torrents As Yet Unknown

CHAPTER ONE

Paradise on the Big Screen

The Indus River

One of us did the cussing, the others prayed.

— DON HATCH

July 11, 1956

From a precarious jeep track hundreds of feet above the white torrent, the Indus River appeared bigger than anything Bus Hatch had ever attempted to raft. Probably bigger than anything *anyone* had attempted to raft. Barren khaki hillsides rose thousands of feet in all directions, rocky ribs exposed above slopes of scree and tangles of low bush so brown as to appear as hard as the rock itself. And just over that immediate horizon, unseen but nevertheless a dominating presence, loomed the icy summits of the greatest mountain ranges on Earth: the Karakorum, the Himalayas, and the Hindu Kush, pumping their glacial meltwater into the Gorges of the Indus.

Less than a month before, the phone had rung in the dusty, cluttered office of Hatch River Expeditions in Vernal, Utah, and the operator announced a call from New York. Bus Hatch, age fifty-six, stocky but athletic, his deeply tanned face accented by round wire-rimmed glasses and gray stubble, listened intently to the voice on the other end of the line, perhaps the best-known voice in the English-speaking world, as the caller made an audacious proposal. Bus spoke little, jotted some notes, and in the end said yes. Replacing the handset in its cradle, he immediately dispatched a substitute trip leader to pull his oldest son, Don, off a raft trip down the Colorado River through the Grand Canyon. Then Bus asked if anyone in the office knew where

Pakistan was. The young country had been part of India when he went
to school.

Now Bus had his answer. At the end of the road for the jeep, in a
tiny village named Gol, Bus, Don, the expedition's leader Otto Lang,
and Pakistani army liaison officer Captain Alim prepared their equipment for a launch early the next morning. Their attempt, if successful,
would be the first known whitewater run in the Himalayas. Hired
village laborers spent hours hand-pumping an enormous inflatable
raft that was twenty-seven feet long and seven and a half feet wide.
One wooden platform spanned the center for an oarsman; another on
the stern mounted a ten-horsepower Johnson outboard motor. Lang
and Captain Alim had no idea what to expect. Bus and Don Hatch
did — perhaps.

The launch point onto any river is a special place. A place to abandon the road, or trail, or whatever line on the map leads back to home
and family and origins. A place to commit to the current that flows
but one direction — into the future. And when that future cannot
be known — not the course of the river, or its dangers — then the
put-in is also a place of fierce anticipation, of dread suppressed, of the
copper taste of adrenaline. A place of voices too loud, jokes too hearty,
the bustle of loading boats exaggerated. The urge is overwhelming to
relieve the tension through action, to launch, even if it is just to round
the next bend and establish the first camp. Yet this gravid moment of
anticipation is also one of the most intense in any explorer's lifetime, a
moment to drink in and savor.

The team launched at 6:45 A.M., and the power of the Indus shocked
even the two whitewater pros. Estimating the size and difficulty
of rapids from hundreds of feet above is notoriously difficult. The
Hatches knew this, of course, even if their companions did not. But
the eye sees what experience leads it to expect, and in the Himalayas,
just as the respiratory system must acclimate to the thin air over a

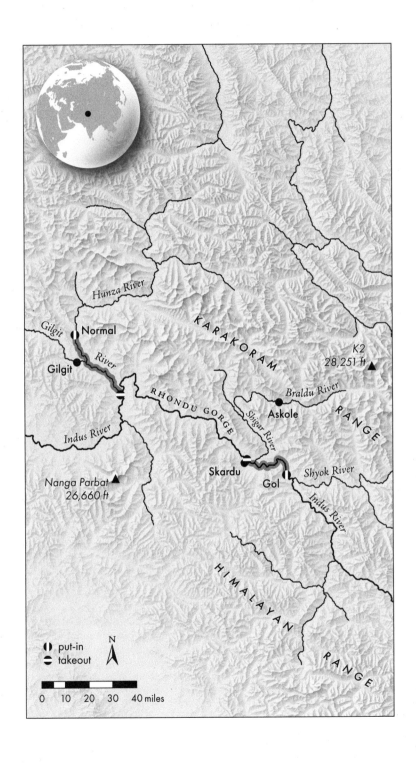

Hunza River

Gilgit

Gilgit
River

Normal

K2
28,251 ft

KARAKORAM

Braldu River

Askole

RANGE

RHONDU GORGE

Shigar River

Indus River

Nanga Parbat
26,660 ft

Skardu

Gol

Shyok River

Indus River

HIMALAYAN

RANGE

put-in
takeout

N

0   10   20   30   40 miles

period of weeks, so too must the eye and brain adapt to the titanic scale. Legendary British climber and explorer Eric Shipton articulated the dynamic in this description from the early days of his landmark 1934 exploration of Nanda Devi with H. W. Tilman: "I was not yet used to the immense scale of the gorge and its surroundings. Tilman suffered from the same complaint. We also had great difficulty in judging the size and angle of minor features . . . However, the eye gradually adjusted itself, and soon we began to move with more confidence."

The glacial meltwaters of the Indus thundered through the canyon at roughly four times the volume of the Colorado that Bus and Don were used to, perhaps a hundred thousand cubic feet per second, and the rapids were steeper and more continuous. As always when nature challenged them, the Hatches deployed their prodigious river skills and cowboy humor. They gritted their teeth but also cursed and laughed to inspire confidence in their nervous passengers.

At one of the rare calm eddies,* beyond which the river narrowed and thundered ominously over a sheer horizon line and plumes of spray shot skyward, evidence of the chaos below, the crew stopped and stepped off the raft for a scouting mission. Edging downstream along the rock wall, Don was dismayed to see the entire river split around a huge boulder then plunge about twenty-five feet in less than thirty

---

* Isaac Newton got it mostly right. Water runs downhill, and rivers flow down to the sea. But in rapids there are two exceptions, where the flow is back upstream. These two features lie at the very core of whitewater river running. An eddy is a roughly horizontal, circular flow on the downstream side of an obstacle blocking the current, usually a rock in midstream or a shoreline protrusion. Water accelerating past the obstacle sucks water from behind it as well, which is then backfilled from water farther downstream, setting up a circular flow. From almost placid pools barely the size of a kayak on smaller rivers to swirling maelstroms hundreds of feet in length with their own whitewater features flowing back upstream, eddies are the whitewater paddlers' refuge from the otherwise relentless flush downstream. Whether you are powering a twenty-seven-foot raft, maneuvering a tiny kayak, or swimming after an accident, these are the spots to catch a breath, to glance over a shoulder to plan the next route, or to get out onto shore. In the most basic terms, running a whitewater river boils down to leaping from one such refuge to the next — "eddy-hopping" in the whitewater lexicon.

yards, careening into the cliff wall on the right and creating a violent recirculating eddy on the left. But they reboarded and went for it.

As the raft hit the point of commitment, Don revved the outboard motor, and they accelerated down the tongue of racing water *"like flies on our way to the sewer."* In the massive white recirculating hole* at the bottom, the raft folded in on itself, launching Lang backward into Don and almost knocking both over the stern. Half full of water, the raft careened toward the rock wall on the right, rode high on the massive pillow of water piling against the cliff face, then slithered along the escarpment to the pool below.

Later that day the raft and its exhausted crew drifted out of the narrow canyon to the wide, flat river by the regional center at Skardu, gateway to the Karakoram mountain range and connected to the rest of Pakistan only by caravan trails and a short military airstrip. Otto Lang cabled back to New York:

> BUS AND DON HATCH MADE THE FIRST DESCENT OF THE INDUS
> GORGES FROM A POINT THIRTY MILES ABOVE SKARDU STOP I
> WAS MERELY A WIDE-EYED PASSENGER AND HAVE RARELY
> WITNESSED SUCH A CATACLYSMIC FORCE OF NATURE, ONLY
> COMPARABLE TO BEING SWEPT AWAY BY AN AVALANCHE STOP

Ironically, no film was shot of that momentous day. Ironic because the expedition for which Don and Bus had been recruited was part of a film shoot. Otto Lang, an immigrant to America from the former

---

* A hole is a roughly vertical, circular flow occurring when water flowing over an under-water obstacle is forced upward into one or more waves. If the upthrust wave is too steep to resist the pull of gravity, it tumbles down into its trough, like an ocean wave breaking as it is forced upward by a shallowing shoreline. Like eddies, this circular flow can stop a boater — but often not in a good way. Riverbeds offer an infinite variety of configurations, of course, but when a wide hole is formed perpendicular to the down-stream current it can recirculate floating objects almost indefinitely, and depending on its size it can be anything from a place for a kayaker to play and show off to a death trap. Also called stoppers or hydraulics, these are not the only hazards on whitewater, but they are probably the most common on the bigger, more difficult rivers.

Austro-Hungarian Empire, had parlayed his status as *the* ski instructor for Hollywood's elite into film-directing opportunities. His team had brought with them to Pakistan the most sophisticated movie cameras of the day, and they were there at the behest of the most famous documentary filmmaker of his generation. No explorer had ever before attempted to raft the remote, gigantic rivers of the Himalaya. The unprecedented effort was the brainchild of Lowell Thomas, the voice on the other end of that telephone call Bus had received from New York just a few weeks earlier.

Thomas was an incongruous product of the rough-edged gold-mining boomtown of Cripple Creek, Colorado. His father, a medical doctor and polymath scholar, drilled into him from childhood the formalities of elocution and oratory. He first made his reputation as a documentary filmmaker and adventure travel celebrity by tracking T. E. Lawrence across the deserts of Arabia during World War I. In the words of Lawrence biographer Malcolm Brown, "Thomas breathlessly portrayed Lawrence's exploits in Arabia through films, radio broadcasts, and print to an audience hungry for victories and heroes during the dark days of the war." He almost single-handedly created the legend of "Lawrence of Arabia," to the introverted scholar's dismay. The flamboyant Thomas emerged from the war in the front ranks of American documentary filmmakers.

In 1930 the young Columbia Broadcasting System aired Thomas's nightly news program, the country's only national radio news show. With his resonant voice yet apolitical, folksy style, he maintained his preeminent position for four decades, with his show moving from CBS to the rival National Broadcasting Company (NBC) and back to CBS again as the news industry grew up around him. His nightly audience was estimated in 1936 to be twenty million, from Canada to the Caribbean. Soon after, Fox Movietone News made him the voice of newsreels in fifteen thousand movie theaters as well.

In the small, clubby society that existed between the world wars, it seemed that Thomas knew personally everyone who mattered. At his elegant five-hundred-acre farm estate on Quaker Hill in the New York Catskills, with its thirty-two-room Georgian mansion house, the political, social, and business elite rubbed shoulders with professional athletes, artists, and European aristocracy. Thomas organized a softball team of neighbors, and visitors like World War I ace Eddie Rickenbacker, world heavyweight boxing champions Gene Tunney and Jack Dempsey, Yankees slugger Babe Ruth, author Dale Carnegie, General Jimmy Doolittle, and New York governor Thomas E. Dewey, for friendly grudge matches against a team that was managed by Franklin D. Roosevelt and composed of the staff, correspondents, and Secret Service detail from his nearby Hyde Park estate. Ike Eisenhower, Richard Nixon, and Sam Snead played Quaker Hill's private golf course. Europe's and America's top alpine skiers congregated on its ski hill.

Eagerly embracing air travel from the earliest days of commercial aviation, Thomas was "jet set" before the jet was invented. No place was too remote, no kingdom too forbidden. He had the connections to wangle invitations and expedite travel for himself and his camera. He toured India with the Prince of Wales, flew to both poles, rode horses over the Himalayan range to Lhasa to visit the Dalai Lama, rode camels across the Sahara to Timbuktu, drove over the legendary Khyber Pass to meet with King Amanullah Khan of Afghanistan in Kabul.

By the 1950s Thomas was heavily invested in a new moviemaking technology, Cinerama — the IMAX of its day. Utilizing a camera that shot simultaneously through three lenses, the film was then projected on a custom-installed curved screen that wrapped 146 degrees around the front of the theater and combined with stereo sound to produce something of a three-dimensional, immersive effect.

When he found himself appointed by President Eisenhower to represent the United States at the coronation of a new king of Nepal in May 1956, Thomas rightly foresaw that this might be a final display of vanishing Oriental splendor in the rapidly modernizing and globalizing

world. He determined to use the occasion to showcase his new technology by displaying the exotic grandeur of the Himalayas and South
Asia. Unlike his previous documentaries and travelogues, his chosen
vehicle this time was to be a dramatic feature film, *Search for Paradise*,
a loosely scripted story of two former American airmen traveling the
world in search of adventure and fulfillment.

In addition to the coronation scene in Kathmandu, a polo tournament in Hunza, exotic temples in Ceylon, and the legendary house-
boats of the Vale of Kashmir, one highlight was to be a whitewater
adventure (initially to be kayaking, later changed to rafting) where the
mighty Indus River carves a cleft between the Himalayan and Karakoram ranges of Pakistan. In 1956 there had been no known whitewater expeditions anywhere in the region, and Lowell Thomas did not
know the first thing about rivers or whitewater. But he did know how
to find his Lawrence.

He recruited one of his skiing pals, former Dartmouth Outing
Club ski racer and pioneer Colorado kayaker Steve Bradley, to fly to
northern Pakistan and scout the river in advance of the film crew. At
the historic Flashman's Hotel in Rawalpindi, Pakistan, Bradley briefed
director Otto Lang on the enormity of his task. Kayaks in 1956 were
still European adaptations of the Arctic hunting boats: a rubberized
canvas skin stretched over a wooden frame. Neither the kayaks nor
the paddlers' skills of the day were remotely capable of withstanding
the crushing power of the rivers where Lang and his crew were head-
ing. And mounted with the massive Cinerama camera, the lightweight
raft Lowell Thomas had shipped out from a New York sporting goods
store could barely stay upright in the hotel swimming pool. Before
flying back to the States, Bradley advised Thomas that their only hope
for success might lie with the legendary river runner Bus Hatch.

Born into a pioneer Mormon family in Vernal, Utah, in 1902, Bus
grew up a skilled hunter, fisherman, boater, and general outdoorsman. He acquired his self-taught whitewater skills through passion,
rawhide toughness, and luck, and when he first ran the Grand Canyon

of the Colorado in 1934, in a wooden dory he had designed and built himself, he was one of the first fifty to do so since Major John Wesley Powell in 1869. Bus was gruff, daring, and self-sufficient. He expected those around him to be the same. Quick to anger when others did not equal his skill and nerve, he also met physical adversities — from wrecking a boat to running out of food or being caught in a winter ice storm — with dry western humor. Crewmen with thick enough skin to stay on with him were intensely loyal.

Initially, fellow river runners were few, and the fragile wooden rowboats used to shoot whitewater rapids were ill suited to the task. The end of World War II, however, brought to market a bonanza of war-surplus rubber assault boats and huge twenty-seven-foot pneumatic pontoons from the floating bridges that conveyed the Allied armies across the rivers of Europe. Bus was quick to appreciate the utility of both on the big, fast rivers of the American West, and he soon had them rigged into craft that could carry not just himself and his fellow rivermen but passengers as well. By the mid-1950s, Hatch River Expeditions, run by Bus, his sons, and other family members, was the premier outfitter taking groups down the Green and Colorado Rivers, the Salmon in Idaho, and other major western rivers. Bus had no peers in big whitewater.

Otto Lang did not return upriver to Gol the next day to repeat for the camera the record-setting run. He concluded that it was too high-risk for his cameras and untrained crew. It was also, frankly, not very photogenic. From the narrow confines of the gorge, not a snowcapped mountain summit could be seen, and the sun reached the river only a few hours daily. Cinematically speaking, they might as well have been rafting through a strip mine. Bus and Don, of course, had made the trip to South Asia for the greatest whitewater adventure of their lives, and they were willing to go back and make the run again. But for producer Thomas and director Lang, the mission was not ultimately

about running a Himalayan river, nor even producing a documentary
film about a whitewater expedition. Rather, their goal was to make
a Hollywood epic about an adventure in the Himalayas that would
showcase Cinerama technology and transport American theater audiences to places beyond their imagination.

In September of the following year, flyers for the film they were
making would shout in bold type outside its world premiere at the
Warner Theatre in New York: "DREAM NO MORE . . . now you can
LIVE it through CINERAMA! LIVE the thunderous, swirling ride down
the murderous rapids of the unconquered Indus River in a frail
rubber raft!"

The crew reloaded all of their equipment into a Pakistan Air
DC-3 and relocated ninety miles northwest to Gilgit. Almost a week
of splendid river running on two tributaries of the Indus followed.
Starting above the village of Nomal on two black rafts, one a large
pontoon boat with a platform for the three-lens Cinerama camera and
the second a smaller rubber assault boat, they filmed roughly a dozen
whitewater miles of the Hunza River to its confluence with the larger
Gilgit River.

After the Hunza joined the Gilgit, the combined flow nearly
matched what they had experienced on the Indus at Skardu. The
canyon was less constricted, however, and the vistas of distant mountains more photogenic. They encountered huge waves and recirculating holes like ocean breakers where the current poured over
massive submerged boulders. Assistant cameraman Jack Priestly was
so unnerved by the pounding whitewater that he refused to rejoin
the rafting team after a break. The crew was across the river from
the trail and base camp when he made his decision, and he had to
be talked into reluctantly reboarding the raft so he could be ferried
across the river.

The Gilgit flowed into the Indus well downstream from Skardu,
and beyond the confluence of the two mighty rivers the rafts proceeded
on a flow almost double that above, in a canyon vast almost beyond

imagination. British historian John Keay had described the canyon decades earlier:

> There is something distinctly other-worldly about its horrify-
> ing emptiness. Save for the dramatic changes in temperature the
> seasons pass unnoticed; rainfall is negligible, vegetation non-
> existent. The scenery, if one can call it that, is a testimony less to
> the gentle forces of nature than to sudden primordial upheavals.
> Seismic rumbles set the crags oscillating; cataclysms scour out
> the defiles. When earlier in the [nineteenth] century, a chunk
> of Nanga Parbat fell across the river, it dammed it to a depth of
> a hundred fathoms and the lake tailed almost to Gilgit; when
> it broke, a Sikh army camped two hundred miles away in the
> Punjab had been wiped out.

Over a driftwood fire, Bus Hatch grilled chops for the entire party — a last-night-on-the-river hallmark of Colorado, Green, and Yampa river raft trips. It was July 19, 1956, and the following morning they would take a final run down the Indus, filming a climactic sequence of running the rapids of the Indus with Himalayan glaciers filling the sky above. After that, Bus and Don would return to their familiar high plateaus and canyonlands of the American Southwest. The film crew would move on to their next shooting location in Ceylon (Sri Lanka).

The swollen river raced past camp, roiling with glacial meltwater, gritty with glacial scour. Random boils formed, whirled downstream a few yards, disappeared again with a hiss. If he listened carefully, Jim Parker, who was with the expedition as an actor, could hear a faint cracking sound, like billiard balls colliding, as stones rolled along the riverbed. Just downstream, Mount Nanga Parbat, westernmost and cruelest of the Himalayas' eight-thousand-meter giants, soared implausibly high in the sky, gleaming white in the setting sun. Parker's heart and soul soared with it.

At forty-five Parker was not the expedition's youngest member, but he was perhaps its freest spirit. Tall and athletic, with chiseled features, high forehead, and dark good looks, the Colorado outdoorsman and athlete had tried his hand at acting as a full-time career and was still a member of the Screen Actors Guild, but the glamor of Tinseltown had worn thin. He had become a professional ski instructor on Mount Rainier, and in Pakistan he discovered mountains that moved him deeply. As the others celebrated their last night on the river and talked of the luxuries awaiting them in Rawalpindi, Parker confided reflectively to his companions: "I love this mountain and countryside so much, I wouldn't mind at all if I spent the rest of my life here."

One regret was that he had not been given the chance to ride the great black pontoon raft pulled up beside their camp during their time on the Hunza, Gilgit, and Indus Rivers. A skiing pal of Lowell Thomas, he would appear in other segments of the film. Each day he importuned the expedition leaders, and each day he was told that every one of the six-man crew had a particular task, that there was no place in the plan for a seventh. There was not even a spare life jacket.

There was an extra fervor about the sand beach that final morning of the shoot, the scheduled wrap. Work crews pumped air to stiffen the two black rafts, warmed up the two outboard motors mounted on the stern of the camera raft, filled jugs of drinking water and tied them securely aboard. Cameramen mounted the great, three-lens Cinerama camera to its platform, loaded its reels of unexposed film, then adjusted its waterproof housing. The designated crewmen tied, and then retied, their life jackets.

But this morning, master cameraman Harry Squire had fallen ill, so Lang finally granted Jim Parker's wish, subbing him in as the sixth and final member of the pontoon raft crew.

The stage was set. Nanga Parbat loomed high and white in the cloudless sky. Just downstream, the swift Indus plunged into a large, boiling white rapid. The players stood in the wings. Don was to run first, rowing the smaller assault raft alone. The large, camera-mounted pontoon raft commanded by Bus would follow closely, filming Don's run with Nanga Parbat in the frame. With that final, climactic scene, Lang would have the entire whitewater rafting sequence in the can; the production unit could grab a few days' R&R in Rawalpindi, then move on to their final location.

"Short timer's attitude," soldiers call it, those manic, unbidden swings from fearful overcaution to reckless abandon as the days count down to the end of a combat tour. The rafters were not in combat, of course, but they had spent weeks in stressful confrontation with the three rivers, in a harsh land profoundly alien to most of them. Looking back forty years later, Otto Lang mused, "Maybe we were all too excited that it was all over; maybe our very strict cautionary measures were neglected."

Preoccupied with last-minute details of the launch, Lang was not aware when former assistant cameraman Jack Priestly, who had begged off riding the raft days before, clambered aboard, declared his intent to replace the ailing Harry Squire, and claimed the life jacket Jim Parker wore. Parker yielded up the life jacket, but not his last chance to ride the raft. He settled himself inconspicuously, the seventh member of a six-man crew.

From the launch site, the rapid ahead looked routine. The rafts moved slowly across the backwater close to the beach, then accelerated as they hit the main stream, hurtling one behind the other toward the whitewater, Bus feathering with oars and outboard motors to keep Don and the smaller raft in front of the camera. Approaching the entrance to the rapid, the lead raft suddenly slowed its momentum as Don discovered that one of his oars was bad and paused to mount a spare. To avoid plowing him under, Bus signaled his motormen to swing the huge raft to the left.

And then one of the outboard motors quit — the first such incident on the whole trip. Unable to straighten or regain momentum, the mammoth raft — twenty-seven feet long, seven and a half feet wide, more than a ton of neoprene and canvas, camera, motors, and crew — slid awkwardly into a huge recirculating hole.

When the wheels come off in any fast-moving, adrenaline-fueled event, different participants remember different, often conflicting, details. Tunnel vision, selective memory, even short-term amnesia are to be expected.

Otto Lang recalled the entire large pontoon raft being tossed within seconds into the air "like a child's toy" and seeing nothing but the camera high above his head in a torrent of foaming water.

To Bus Hatch, the raft seemed to roll in slow motion, and "easy as anything" he found himself in a fight for his life, trapped in the dark under the capsized boat with a rope tightly half-hitched above his knee. By curling up in a ball he was able to catch gasps of air on the crests of standing waves. Eventually he worked his badly wrenched leg out of its snare and struggled to shore with four of the crew and the capsized raft. Jim Parker and Pete Passos from the production crew were missing. A check under the raft revealed no one — and no camera.

After seating his new oar, Don Hatch had pulled left and found a clean line down the long rapid. Maintaining his concentration downstream, the first sign of trouble he saw from the trailing raft was a train of gas cans and oars floating by when he reached an eddy. Pete Passos then appeared, and Don picked him up. Pete and Jim Parker had been tossed together off the port side of the raft, and they had surfaced clinging together. The next churning wave submerged and separated them. Don watched the water for signs of Jim, but saw none.

The distraught team members scrambled downstream along the shoreline, shouting Jim's name, searching for any trace, as far as the next big rapid. There, they reluctantly conceded, no swimmer could possibly survive, especially with no life jacket or protection from hypothermia.

Back in New York a stunned Lowell Thomas led his nightly radio news broadcast with a tribute to James Parker and dispatched the following telegram for delivery to Otto Lang and the grieving expedition team upon their return to Rawalpindi:

DEEPLY SADDENED AND SHOCKED BY JIM'S TRAGIC DEATH AND
FULLY SHARE YOUR GRIEF STOP WILL GET IN TOUCH WITH HIS
MOTHER AND BROTHER STOP SUGGEST ALL OF YOU RETURN
HOME EARLIEST POSSIBLE WITH GLOBEMASTER STOP IF ANY
MEMBER OF CREW IN DISTRESS SEND HOME BY COMMERCIAL
AIRLINER STOP UPON YOUR RETURN ALL OF US TOGETHER
CAN FORMULATE PLANS TO COMPLETE PICTURE STOP

After a few days of recuperation in Rawalpindi, however, and a sorrowful wake for Jim Parker, the production crew, under Lang's leadership, elected to carry on with filming the last sequence on location in Ceylon with their spare camera, rewriting the script to account for Parker's absence. The Hatches, Bus's knee still badly wrenched from his swim and Don stricken by typhoid from river water, convalesced for two weeks in a Rawalpindi hospital before flying home, beaten up but mission accomplished.

Through the fall and winter Lowell Thomas and his production staff in New York stitched together the Cinerama extravaganza. Visuals from the three-eyed camera on location in Nepal, Kashmir, Hunza, the Indus, and Ceylon were painstakingly synced with narration throughout by Thomas himself. For the special 360-degree theater speakers, the Oscar-winning composing team of Dimitri Tiomkin (music) and Ned Washington (lyrics), who are best known for "Do Not Forsake Me, Oh My Darlin'" from *High Noon*, recorded the musical score in Carnegie Hall to capture its superior acoustics.

Publicity and fanfare leading up to the September 1957 world premiere in New York City were grand. Lowell flew Bus and Don from Utah, had them inducted into the Explorers Club, and paraded them down the East River in a pontoon raft full of waving bathing beauties. Members of the audience inside the theater were issued life jackets and doused with buckets of water from the balconies during the rafting sequences. Neither before nor since has river exploration been subject to such spectacle.

Yet for all the hype, Thomas had decided from the beginning that the death of Jim Parker was not to be exploited. He had eulogized his skiing friend on the national news right after the accident and had a memorial plaque mounted by the Rakhiot Bridge over the Indus at the base of Nanga Parbat, beside those of the thirty-one climbers who had died on the mountain to that date. But in the program for the movie premiere, the only indication of the actor's death was the use of the past tense in his brief bio.

And then the critics panned *Search for Paradise*. Thomas had spent his career at the very pinnacle of documentary, travelogue, and newsreel filmmaking. In Hollywood he championed the idea that "Cinerama was — and is — ideal for nonfiction because it gives the audience the unique experience of actual participation." But his attempt to meld his favorite medium with a thin veneer of story line and acting produced neither compelling story nor convincing documentary.

The Hatches and Otto Lang's production crew accomplished an astonishing feat for the mid-1950s: the first ever whitewater rafting in the Himalayas, with first descents on three different rivers. Yet in the final cut not a single raft running rapids was to be seen — not Don Hatch leading the way in his oar rig, not the pontoon raft and crew as would be seen by the motormen in the back, not the actors who supposedly were carrying the story arc. Just waves, splashing into and over the Cinerama camera mounted on the very front, without points of reference or scale. The inconceivable proportions of Himalayan mountains and rivers might have been better portrayed had the Cinerama screen curled up over the audience's heads rather than around the sides.

Although Lowell Thomas's narration implied that all the river action portrayed in *Search for Paradise* had taken place on the Indus, in fact the expedition's two days of high drama on that river were entirely absent. The first day's warm-up above Skardu was never filmed, and on the last, fatal day the camera was lost along with Jim Parker. The roller-coaster effect of selected footage on the Hunza and Gilgit Rivers did enjoy some popularity with theater audiences, but the missed opportunity, both for documentary filmmaking and the history of whitewater exploration, was immense.

After the premiere, Bus and Don Hatch returned to Utah as the first ever to run rivers in the Himalayas, legends in the exclusive fraternity of Colorado River guides. Ten years later, in 1967, international river rafting pioneer and author Richard Bangs graduated high school in Virginia and went west with dreams of becoming a Grand Canyon guide:

> I was nineteen. Bus Hatch had died a couple of years earlier, and now Don and Ted, his two sons, ran the business. Sometimes late at night, with campfire shadows dancing on the canyon wall, talk would turn to Don's Indus expedition. None of the guides knew the full story, just tidbits dropped by Don at the office, the bar, or the put-in. He didn't talk much about it, but enough for the stuff of a legend. "I'd give my right oar to row the Indus," a guide once told me. And whenever I'd screw up in a rapid, break a frame, wash a passenger overboard, or simply scare myself with a close call, I'd say to myself, *Don ran the Indus — ten times the size of the Colorado, three times the speed, and cold as winter.*

CHAPTER TWO

To Get Away from England

The Inn, Colorado, and Blue Nile Rivers

> For more than two hundred years now Englishmen have
> been wandering about the world for their amusement . . .
> The Scotch endured great hardships in the cause of com-
> merce; the French in the cause of either power or evan-
> gelism. The English only have half (and wholly) killed
> themselves in order to get away from England.
>
> — EVELYN WAUGH

Chris Bonington had his doubts about how this enterprise would
turn out. The veteran mountaineer and *Daily Telegraph* writer
admired the enthusiasm and boating skills of the five young British
kayakers gathered in a meadow on the left bank of the Inn River —
enough so that he had convinced his editor to sponsor their dream
of kayaking (equally referred to as canoeing in Great Britain) the
length of the Inn in Switzerland and to send him along as photo-
journalist. He believed this whitewater run to be a challenge "equiv-
alent to climbing the North Wall of the Eiger," a feat Bonington had
been the first Briton to achieve. Before they launched downstream
into the first of the Inn's whitewater gorges, he suggested they spend
a day warming up, testing equipment, and shooting photos at one of
the rare rapids that was handy to the road, where access and rescue
were easy.

It was a spectacular setting on that warm August afternoon in
1969. Golden hayfields, punctuated by tidy farmyards and cottages
with ornate wooden balconies, rose steeply to the evergreen flanks of

the soaring Swiss Alps. Goats bounded across the narrow road as a
five-car railroad train clattered down the Inn River Valley. Fat milk
cows posed as if for a thousand chocolate bar wrappers, and the sun
glinted off the swiftly moving water. The paddlers responded eagerly
to Bonington's suggestion of a warm-up run, surfing across a train of
six-foot waves, capsizing and Eskimo rolling* their watertight boats
back upright, tucking nimbly into the eddies behind rocks to stop,
carrying their lightweight, fragile boats back up the open shoreline
time and again to show off their skills to Bonington's camera and to a
growing crowd of amazed Swiss onlookers. Two girlfriends passed a
hat and collected that night's beer money.

Yet just downstream, all knew, lay a darker, colder world. Five times
between its headwaters near St. Moritz and the Austrian border, the
Inn River severed its link to the road leading down its bucolic valley.
Dank walls of mossy rock and tangles of stunted evergreens closed in
on either side. The Inn surged down into narrow, shadowed gorges,
accelerated around tumbled boulders and uprooted trees, leaped
whitely over rock ledges, and roared its frustration at obstacles to its
descent through the heart of the Alps.

Jeff Slater, leader of the kayakers, had spent the previous summer
kayaking in the Alps with German and Austrian river runners,
from whom he heard tales of the Inn's canyons. Only three of the
five in Switzerland had been previously run; another had been
attempted, with two deaths the result. Slater and his four teammates were about to attempt to run all five, from top to bottom,
seventy miles in total. The paddlers were warmed up and ready to
begin the adventure — and the *Daily Telegraph* had in the can both
portrait and action shots of each kayaker, the foundation for any
story, any outcome.

---

* A technique of righting a capsized kayak by twisting the paddle to raise the paddler's
body back to an upright position without exiting the boat.

Weeks before, in Yorkshire, the excited expedition team had milled about, lashing boats and baggage onto their shiny new microbus and trailer. On either side of the van's roof rack, signs a foot high and almost the length of a kayak displayed colorful Union Jacks and proclaimed this to be THE ALPINE CANOEING GROUP — RIVER INN EXPEDI-TION. An equally new trailer behind, stacked high with ten shiny new, brightly colored fiberglass kayaks, displayed the same Union Jack and announced: CANOE CENTRESPORT — LEEDS.

All this display — the media attention, the sponsorship, a support team of rescue climbers and drivers — was, to organizer and leader Slater's bemusement, "a complete accident." After his eye-opening summer in the Alps in 1968, he was eager to return in 1969 to try the Inn and other rivers. But the British economy was facing hard times. In addition to low wages, to prevent currency drain citizens were limited to taking no more than sixty-five pounds when they traveled to the Continent for tourism. Also, the world whitewater champion-ships were to be held that summer in Bourg-Saint-Maurice, France, and the focus of most of Britain's top paddlers lay there. With summer fast approaching, only Trevor Eastwood had committed to join Jeff to explore Alpine rivers.

Until, that is, Trevor conceived the notion, after attending a lecture by Chris Bonington, to call it not a paddling holiday but to use the mountaineering term *expedition*. Set a challenging objective, gener-ate media interest, find sponsors, enlist a team. Eastwood and Slater captured Bonington's imagination with a kayaking demonstration at the handy and accessible Linton Falls rapids in Yorkshire, and to Slat-er's amazement the River Inn Expedition became reality within weeks. The Alpine Canoeing Group, made up of just Slater and Eastwood, printed letterhead stationery. Equipment sponsors and the *Daily Telegraph* fell into place. Kayakers Lindsay Williams and Dave Allen joined up, as did Dave Clarke and fellow climbers Ralph Heather-ington and Barry Paige to provide support and rescue. Paige's wife,

Jeannie, and Slater's future wife, Helen Mortimer, volunteered for base camp support.

When a dusty green Ford Cortina pulled up to drop off the fifth paddler, Mike Jones, straight from high school, Jeff wondered yet again about his judgment in accepting the talented but young and inexperienced final paddler to the group and about his parents' judgment in allowing him to join. With his Beatles mop, slight Mick Jagger pout, and skinny frame, Mike could have been fifteen instead of his actual seventeen. When he emerged from his parents' car, his loud checked trousers demanded attention — and got it. Trevor Eastwood looked up and announced to all that "Rupert" had arrived, a reference to a cartoon bear who appeared daily in the newspapers in similar pants. The name would stick, not just within this group and for this expedition, but for the rest of Mike's paddling career. It became "Hey, Rupert, another beer here!" and "Rupert, where's my tea?" as Mike accepted with good humor the ragging that came with his junior status.

Slater spent the morning following the initial warm-up session in Switzerland with Bonington and the climbers establishing camera positions in the Brail, first of the Inn River gorges. In what would become the expedition's routine, they set ropes for access up and down the steep gorge walls and determined a detailed timeline when the kayakers were to reach each spot. Although at nineteen Slater was only two years older than Mike Jones, he'd spent those extra years maturing at university and running rivers in the Alps. The expedition was the product of his imagination and organization, and the others readily acknowledged his leadership both on and off the water.

Shortly after noon, Slater was the first of the paddlers to enter the unknown, three-mile-long slot, and immediately he realized he "had certainly never been down anything like it" in his life. The Inn was narrow within its constraining walls, steep, and continuous, with few eddies or pools in which to catch his breath or consider his route

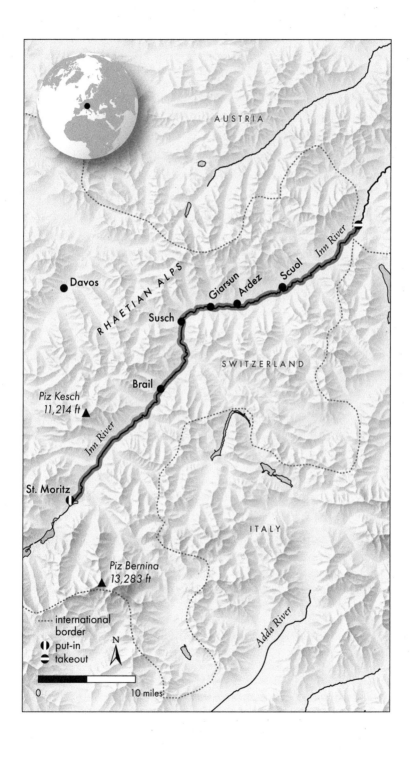

AUSTRIA

Davos

RHAETIAN ALPS

Giarsun
Ardez
Scuol

Inn River

Susch

SWITZERLAND

Brail

Piz Kesch
11,214 ft

Inn River

St. Moritz

ITALY

Piz Bernina
13,283 ft

---- international
border
put-in
takeout
N

0   10 miles

Adda River

downstream. In the first long rapid, he capsized in the final drop but rolled up safely.

Following next, twenty-two-year-old schoolteacher Lindsay Williams rolled twice, and in that loss of control his boat broached on a rock and was badly damaged. Since this was just the entrance rapid to the gorge, the support crew was able to provide a spare boat. Dave Allen, Trevor Eastwood, and Rupert followed in that order and made it down unscathed. All fought through the second series of big drops, but they were a sober and big-eyed group as they bobbed in small eddies next to shore and caught their breath. Over the mossy boulders they held to steady their restless kayaks, the water crept higher from morning snowmelt high in the surrounding mountains, and beneath their hulls rumbled dislodged rocks washing downstream.

Always intense, and disconcerted by the unfamiliar fit and performance of his replacement kayak, Williams soon had more problems, capsized, and this time had to swim. Seeing his predicament from upstream, Eastwood hastily pulled his kayak ashore and pelted downstream on foot to help. Williams barely managed to swim to shore before his swamped boat washed over the next big drop and was torn apart. As, to Eastwood's dismay, was his own — dislodged from its perch on the bank by the rising meltwater. Isolated on the right bank, opposite the road and campsite, Eastwood tied into a climbing rope for a tricky swim and pendulum across the icy current. Water streaming from his curly brown hair and Viking beard, despondent over his failure to finish the first challenge of the Inn, yet somewhere deep within relieved that the stress was over, he joined Williams for the arduous scramble up the canyon wall.

Slater, Allen, and Jones worked their way down four more big rapids before emerging from the Brail Gorge. In one violent chute, the seat of Slater's kayak broke free of its attachment to the boat, leaving him sitting awkwardly on the bottom of the hull. He had no choice but to continue, aware that from that loose position he would be unlikely to Eskimo roll should he capsize. After drifting the few miles down the swift but now flatter river to their grassy campground in the village of Susch, Slater realized that to continue they would need to find a new level of paddling, one that none of them had ever before achieved. And after just the first day, they were down from ten boats to just seven — if, that is, he could repair his broken seat.

Camp that evening, following their first encounter with the Inn River gorges, was a heady atmosphere of adrenaline and nervous anticipation of what lay downstream, awash in bottle after bottle of strong Swiss beer. Never able to sit still for long, Dave Clarke organized raucous challenges: climbing contests in the rafters of a nearby pavilion, Frisbee games utilizing camping plates and pot lids. When the horseplay tapered off, Bonington regaled the paddlers with tales of mountaineering adventures in the Alps, Patagonia, and Nepal. He told of accompanying a British army expedition attempting to raft down the Blue Nile in Ethiopia, of cataracts and bandit attacks and crocodiles and a soldier drowned. Rupert listened attentively, drinking it all in and growing up fast.

It was late the next day — four in the afternoon — before Slater led the team downstream into the second unrun gorge, the Giarsun. The day had been consumed by repairing their battered boats, and now the river was at its daily meltwater high, wider than in the Brail, seventy feet at least, bigger and pushier. Seven-foot waves formed below steep chutes between boulders. Williams wisely dropped out almost immediately. His fiberglass repairs to the boat torn apart in the entrance rapid the previous day did not hold. Full of water, it was becoming increasingly unmanageable.

The others pushed on. Dave Allen was the eldest of the paddlers at twenty-six, the only married, family man. Beneath his white helmet, his fine blond hair was already fading at the temples. He was rock-steady, not given to emotion or exaggeration, and in his words, "It got increasingly hard for three-quarters of a mile . . . the river then took a bend and it got even worse . . . it was the heaviest water I have ever seen."

It was somewhere here, Slater thought uneasily, that the two kayakers must have drowned in their attempt two years before.

Bonington and the rescue climbers had worked their way down into the canyon at its biggest rapid, the crux of the run. The lanky, bearded mountaineer seemed to be everywhere, observing everything through the eye of his Nikon and commenting little. Slater was first to appear from upstream, diving cleanly into an eddy above the first drop and spinning to a halt, followed by Allen. With a glance over their shoulders to see their line, they peeled out into the current and powered through the cauldron in what seemed fine style to Bonington.

Not so to Eastwood and Jones, who came into sight thrown too close together, each trying to avoid collision. Unable to stop in time, both were funneled irresistibly into the entrance chute of the rapids. Eastwood capsized at the bottom of the first drop, failed with his Eskimo roll, exited his boat, and swam desperately for the bank. Only the deft throw of a rope by climber Heatherington immediately above the next drop in the steep cascade saved Eastwood from a nasty swim, and perhaps a tragic outcome. Mike Jones managed to stay upright and scrambled his way through the boulder maze to rejoin Slater and Allen in the refuge of a large eddy.

Downstream lay several more difficult passages, with vicious waves throughout, but when the remaining three kayakers reached the bridge and takeout at the foot of the gorge, they had completed the previously unrun sections of the Inn. They had at least the comfort of knowing that what lay ahead had been run successfully by a team of Austrians, although they had assigned it the highest difficulty rating in whitewater, Class VI, meaning "a threat to life for even the best paddlers."

The Alpine Canoeing Group — River Inn Expedition now consisted of three bedraggled kayakers and just four kayaks. Jeff Slater's doubts were growing, and were it not for the *Daily Telegraph*, he might well have packed it in. Instead, the next day he, Allen, and Jones set themselves for one final push to the Austrian border, the expedition's declared objective. In haste to complete their task, and knowing that others had made it through, they scouted what they could see of the final canyons from the road five hundred feet above the river, then launched into the Ardez Gorge.

They were lucky to escape with their lives. Partway down, the three found themselves flying down a suddenly restricted channel, its banks regular and without the shoreline rocks and eddies they relied upon to stop. Raw, scarred earth on either hand revealed that twin landslides had plunged into the gorge, probably very recently, to create this monstrous flume. The accelerating current narrowed to about ten feet; they had no choice but to keep their thirteen-foot kayaks hurtling forward into the unknown. Then they suddenly found themselves launched — in Slater's words, "shot through a fireman's hose" — into a large, perfectly still pool.

Relief, even elation or pride, might come later. Now, as Slater's heartbeat steadied in the still water, fear and recrimination washed over him. In their haste and overconfidence, they had allowed themselves to be drawn into a place beyond their skills, a place where luck and the river had controlled their fate. He must not let that happen again. The camera-and-climbing crew helped the three shaken paddlers carry over the steep, unconsolidated rubble of freshly broken boulders and tortured tree trunks stripped of limbs and bark, past a twenty-foot falls that poured directly into a massive sieve of boulders.

Not far downstream, the canyon walls opened a bit and the rapids relented. Then, without warning, as the paddlers enjoyed the temporary relief of the wider and easier rapids of the Scuol Gorge, the stern fell completely off Slater's kayak. He barely managed to paddle the wallowing, sinking hull to shore, then stood dripping on the bank, examining the torn fiberglass and polyester hole where the last two feet of his boat had been. With a chill, he realized that the major damage must have occurred unnoticed during the dramatic events upstream; then gentle flexing in the last mile or so had served to sever completely the smashed material. And if that had occurred during the wild ride down the landslide flume . . .

At that moment, Slater decided that despite their achievements, boat design and materials were not in 1969 up to the demands of such expedition paddling. And then, after having led his expedition down every inch of the Inn River from its origin at St. Moritz, he became a spectator and watched as Dave Allen and Mike "Rupert" Jones paddled off to complete the last few miles through the Finstermunz Gorge to the Austrian border. He was content, for reasons he has never fully understood, to leave the last remaining new kayak on its trailer.

The headline of Chris Bonington's story in the *Daily Telegraph Magazine* read BEATING THE WHITE WATER. Maybe. Two of the five paddlers had completed the run. Only three of their ten kayaks remained serviceable. The reunited "accidental expedition" loaded up for the twenty-hour drive back to the UK, and although they remained active in canoe sport and climbing, none would undertake further international river expeditions.

Except for Rupert. He had finished the Inn River canyons in the same boat he started with. He had found a new name, a lifetime inspiration and friend in Bonington, and his calling in life.

If Mike "Rupert" Jones was the young and self-effacing "tea boy" of the team of six on the Inn River in 1969, two years later, still gawky and teenaged, he was almost invisible among the crowd of twenty-four mostly British kayak and canoe paddlers that milled about in the desert heat of Lees Ferry at the put-in on the Colorado River above the Grand Canyon in 1971. Currency restrictions had eased, and the Brits were eager to see the world. Led by English kayaker Chris Hawkesworth, the ten-day, 224-mile run was a first for the British, but hardly a first descent or exploration — part expedition, part tour. Hatch River Expeditions provided five guides and three support rafts, much the same large, motorized rafts Bus and Don had used on the Indus and to run tourists down the Colorado for two decades. California kayaker Art Vitarelli, who had already run the canyon three times, joined the visitors from the UK.

The British undertaking was nevertheless ambitious. The half dozen biggest rapids on the run were the top end of high-volume, powerful rapids then being attempted in small fiberglass kayaks and decked canoes. The silty red Colorado poured through the Grand Canyon at more than ten times the volume of Alpine rivers, or of the revolutionary man-made whitewater course then being built for the Munich Olympics. And while not as steep or boulder-choked, when the Colorado's fifteen to twenty thousand cubic feet of water per second thundered over granite ledges, it formed huge rapids where the power of the water itself, not rocks, posed the greatest risk and challenge. *Canoeing Magazine* editor Mike Clark wrote the following about the first of the significant rapids the Brits faced, Soap Creek, just eleven miles into the run:

> The kayakists were dwarfed by both cliffs and water. It seemed that each craft had to paddle uphill to pull over the peaks of the mighty waves. For seconds the waves would roll back on themselves forming what the white water paddler calls a "stopper." These were real stoppers — going through such waves the kayaks were almost stopped dead and for many such an experience was to be avoided. Kayaks would break through the tip of the waves, then there was a mad dash down into the trough, followed by a beat up the next wave and over the top. At times the kayakists would disappear altogether, or just a blade or crash helmet could be seen as they took on the big water. Suddenly the wave would burst and the paddler race out looking for the next hazard. Thus for a few seconds the waves

would be great stoppers, then giant exploding waves, water
bursting from their tops as if pushed up into the air by some
unseen hand. This was rapid river running at its very best and
certainly for the kayakists it was water almost to the very limits
of paddling ability.

More would come, and bigger. But with each day, each passing mile,
the paddlers became more accustomed to the awesome power of the
water, more confident. This was why they had come. Twenty-five-year-
old Pauline Squires would become the first woman to kayak the entire
run. The following year she represented Great Britain in whitewater
slalom at the Munich Olympics, and four years later she did the same
in flatwater sprint at Montreal. Pauline's future husband, Jon Good-
win, and his paddling partner Albert Woods likewise became the first
tandem canoe team to accomplish the feat, albeit with a dramatic swim
and an even more heroic overnight boat repair to stay in the hunt. Jon
would also join Pauline on the British team in Munich, with a different partner. Albert missed making the Olympic team but years later
was knighted by the queen for his lifetime contributions to British and
European canoe sports.

    And what of Mike Jones? His shy smile, his red-and-yellow kayak,
his battered hockey helmet patched with duct tape appeared in none of
the many photographs illustrating Mike Clark's thirty-four-page special
report in *Canoeing Magazine*. His name appeared only twice: in a list
of all the paddlers and the type of boat each used, and as one of fourteen paddlers to run Crystal Falls (one of the two or three most difficult
rapids in the canyon). And in the forty-two-minute film made by Chris
Hawkesworth, he appears just three times, for a total of fifty seconds:
twice paddling smoothly through big wave trains, once hitching a ride
across a pool on the side of a raft. No fuss, no drama; he was an easy
traveling companion and a paddler capable to the point of being boring.

    However, although not yet twenty, and just beginning his medical stud-
ies at Birmingham University, Mike had already run the Inn, compared

to the North Face of the Eiger for steep, technical Alpine paddling, and now the Grand Canyon, considered the gold standard for big, powerful western US river running. Two vastly different expeditions — in size, in purpose, and in leadership under Jeff Slater and Chris Hawkesworth, respectively. For some, the Olympics were calling — but Rupert had other plans.

Mike turned twenty-one bivouacked in a rocky streambed, sitting back-to-back with Mick Hopkinson, each clutching a pistol and staring out into the Ethiopian night in fear of bandits. Exhausted from running miles of unknown whitewater, some of it blind, and long days on starvation rations, both men eventually dozed into restless sleep. Mike woke at dawn to find the barrel of his Webley revolver pointed directly at his sleeping companion, his forefinger still wrapped around the trigger. Their tumultuous partnership was nevertheless to last across years and continents.

With vehement modesty, Chris Bonington denies being a mentor to Jones. Without doubt, though, he was an inspiration and a lifelong friend. When Mike determined to strike out leading his own kayak expedition, it was the tales of adventure and misadventure on the Blue Nile that Chris had spun over the campfires beside the Inn in 1969 that had captured his ambition. This eastern tributary of the Nile flowed nine hundred miles from the Ethiopian highlands to join the White Nile at Khartoum, over cataracts and through whitewater gorges never attempted, between banks inhabited by armed bandits, across deep pools patrolled by crocodiles longer than a kayak.

This was a somewhat known quantity, but a daunting one. The earliest attempts concentrated on the lower two-thirds of the river, from the Shafartak Bridge, where a road to Addis Ababa crosses the river, below which the gorges are wider and the rapids not so severe. A 1903 expedition nevertheless lost their steel boats in the first cataract they encountered. An eccentric Austrian sculptor on

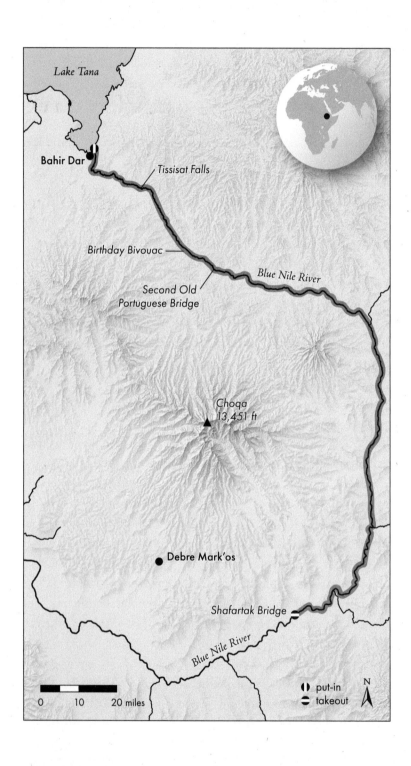

a raft of oil drums met the same fate. A team of Swiss kayakers in 1962 ran most of this section, making it almost to the Sudanese border before being attacked by bandits. Two were killed; the rest barely escaped.

Two years later Swedish kayaker Arne Robin created the model that Jones and Hopkinson would adopt. Paddling solo, camping after dark and departing at daylight, never building a fire, he made it from the Shafartak Bridge to Khartoum in the Sudan in just eight days. Alpine style in its purest form.* Robin returned in 1966 with partner Carl Gustav Forsmark to attempt the upper river, from its source at Lake Tana to the Shafartak Bridge, to complete his success. Their tandem kayak was no match for the big whitewater and cataracts of this never-attempted section. They made barely fifteen miles before nearly drowning and abandoning their effort.

Then in 1968 came the lavish British military expedition that Bonington had accompanied. Captain John Blashford-Snell commanded, apparently more at home in the nineteenth century than the twentieth with his white pith helmet, his ruddy face and narrow mustache, his badges of rank and Sam Brown belt with sidearm. Fifty-six men (mostly in support), three small rubber rafts for the upper, whitewater segment, motorized army assault boats for the

---

* From the earliest days of British attempts to climb Everest, at the instigation of Royal Geographical Society chairman Lieutenant Colonel Sir Francis Younghusband, military planning dominated Himalayan climbing. Armies of Sherpa porters, base camps resembling small cities, and military-style chain of command were the rule right up to, and including, the successful climb in 1953 that summited Edmund Hillary and Tenzing Norgay but was led by Brigadier Sir John Hunt. By the 1930s, however, a counterculture began to emerge, pioneered by H. W. Tilman and Eric Shipton, who disparaged the former approach as "siege tactics." In contrast, they demonstrated the utility of an "Alpine style," climbing with smaller, self-contained parties as mountaineering had evolved in the Swiss Alps. Over the course of several expeditions in the Himalayas and the Karakoram, Tilman and Shipton proved they could travel quickly and lightly through a landscape their predecessors had treated as alien and hostile territory. The price they paid for this speed and freedom lay in greater exposure. More recently, a few transcendent climbers, such as Reinhold Messner, have carried this approach to its logical conclusion with unsupported solo ascents of Mount Everest and other major summits.

lower. A fleet of Land Rovers, a base radio station communicating all the way back to Britain, a single-engine Beaver bush plane. This was mountaineering "siege tactics" adapted to river exploration. After the expedition Blashford-Snell's claims of success rang hollow. They had carried their inadequate rafts around the whitewater upper canyons, and even in doing so had drowned Corporal Ian Macleod, detailed from the Special Air Service commandos, due to their lack of understanding of safe rope handling in swift water. On the lower river their large military party was caught by surprise and ignominiously run off downstream by lightly armed bandits.

To the increasingly confident and bold Mike Jones, the Blue Nile not only conjured all the romance of British nineteenth-century exploration of Africa but also offered a visionary, even evangelical, opportunity to prove the superiority of lightweight, nimble kayaks and small, Alpine-style teams. With introductions and support from Chris Bonington, Mike obtained a fellowship from the Winston Churchill Trust, a foundation that awards overseas research grants to UK citizens "chosen not for their past achievements, but for the power of their ideas and their potential to be change-makers."

The unknown cascades, the crocodiles, and the bandits would be both daunting and thrilling. First, though, the novice expedition leader had to cut his teeth on the financial, logistical, and political challenges of mounting an expedition beyond Europe or North America — a feat almost unheard of in the whitewater world of that era. His bold plans were almost undone even before they reached the Nile.

Captain Blashford-Snell took umbrage at the assertion that the brash university undergraduate could do what his elaborate army expedition had not. He and his military associates discouraged potential sponsors, and two of Britain's strongest paddlers, both military, were refused leave to join Mike's team by their commanders. Discouraged, trip leader and filmmaker from the Grand Canyon expedition, Chris Hawkesworth, also dropped out. Just three weeks before their scheduled departure from the United Kingdom, Mike's expedition team was reduced to three: himself; Mick Hopkinson, who was one of Britain's best river running kayakers; and Glen Greer, whose role would be to provide base radio and shore support.

Stunned, they nonetheless persevered. Mike hastily recruited Steve Nash and Dave Burkinshaw, racers he knew from the slalom world but with whom he had never run a river. Then on July 24, 1972, Mike flew to Africa, deputizing Hopkinson to organize the remaining supplies and follow on.

Landing in Cairo with the remaining team members and supplies two weeks after Mike, Mick's relief at finally arriving in Africa turned to dismay. Their kayaks sat in a lockup beside the airport runway, their shiny hulls already accumulating a layer of African dust. Mike, it seemed, had gone on to Addis Ababa without mentioning that the thirteen-foot craft could not be fit into the cargo hold of the Comet jet that was to fly their last leg. When the desperate paddlers failed to force the kayaks through the passenger door and began trying to remove a window, the exasperated pilot took off, leaving team, kayaks, and supplies abandoned on the Cairo runway. Only their leader had made it to the right country.

Following days of pleading phone calls, an Ethiopian cargo aircraft finally saw the rest of the team to Addis Ababa, but their first day on the Blue Nile revealed that they were by no means united. Frustrated by the many delays, Mike plunged forward, heedless of the concerns of Steve and Dave, whose very different, and more deliberate, vision for the expedition called for testing radios and other equipment and time-consuming scouting of the whitewater from shore. Two acrimonious days later, Steve and Dave were trekking overland with porters some thirty miles to the beginning of the lower river, as Mike and Mick launched into the unknown canyons of the Upper Blue Nile and Glen monitored progress on the base radio.

Constrained between looming walls of black basalt and swollen by monsoon rains, the brick-red river tore around corners and pulsed over blind ledges. Mike and his kayak were sucked completely underwater in one monstrous boil. Convinced that no rescue of a swimmer would be possible, that it would mean certain death, the paddlers wedged themselves irrevocably into their boats, Mike with his 16mm Bolex film camera, Mick with their shortwave radio, and committed themselves downstream. They were fortunately able to see in advance and carry around a two-mile-long defile where Hopkinson estimated the river raged no more than six or seven feet wide.

That night, September 6, 1972, the night of Mike's birthday bivouac, PLO terrorists stormed Olympic Village in Munich, killed two members of the Israeli team, and held nine others hostage.

The following afternoon, the two paddlers emerged from the canyons, and the Blue Nile mellowed to easy rapids and riffles separated by languid pools. Rejoined after their respective ordeals running the whitewater canyons and bushwhacking cross-country, the original group of four kayakers — Mike, Mick, Steve, and Dave — drifted downstream.

A large crocodile slithered down the bank into a shoreline eddy, peeled out into the current, and swam purposely toward the four kayaks. Hastily ripping off their spray decks, Mick scrambled for his pistol, Mike for his movie camera. When the croc was about twenty feet away and about to submerge for its final underwater approach, Mick aimed his revolver over his bow so the recoil of the .45-caliber Webley would blow the boat backward rather than capsize him, then shot the croc between its eyes.

As the croc sank from sight beneath the muddy water, Mike exploded in frustrated anger. He had been unable to assemble the camera in time and had entirely missed filming the incident. He had failed to capture on film the spectacular whitewater action upstream, when he and Mick had been pushed to their limit. Now he was determined to return at least with sensational footage of crocodile encounters.

He announced his plan. When the crocs submerged, they always surfaced again at the kayaker's last-seen position in the drifting current. If the kayaks immediately paddled off at right angles, the croc would emerge close, but off the mark. It would submerge again, and the high-stakes game of marco-polo would repeat. That should give Mike enough time to film. The very next croc failed to read the script. It surfaced immediately beside Mick's kayak; he shot one-handed across his body, narrowly avoiding being capsized. Mick, Steve, and Dave revolted. Attempts to get crocodiles to perform for Mike's camera were over.

The following day, the paddlers arrived at the Shafartak highway bridge, starting point for previous descents of the lower river, and the team members were torn about proceeding. Mike was not one to abandon his announced plan to kayak the entire river, and he still did not have satisfactory film documenting the adventure. On the other hand, he and Mick had completed their first descent of the upper river — and proved, he felt, the superiority of their nimble whitewater craft. Steve and Dave were unenthusiastic about the crocodiles, but they had come all the way to Africa and had barely paddled two days.

Into the endless loop of opinions and desires, Mick Hopkinson interjected quantitative analyses. Two Webley .45 revolvers were their only effective defense against the crocodiles. From the put-in at Lake Tana they had fired to date forty-seven rounds of ammunition in 220 river miles — most expended in the past two days. They had remaining fifty-three waterlogged rounds, and four hundred miles of croc-and-bandit-infested river to Sudan. The deeply fragmented expedition declared victory and returned to England.

Brooding over the disparate paddlers' failure to share his vision and his tolerance of risk; his own failure to capture on film the imagery necessary to impress the sponsors of this and, more important, future expeditions; and their foreshortened ending, which offered no unequivocal victory over Captain Blashford-Snell and the military forces that had so frustrated his plans, Rupert barely spoke during the journey home. Next time would be different!

It would be four years before he launched his next expedition.

CHAPTER THREE

To Dare

The Dudh Kosi River

It is not because things are difficult that we do not dare; it
is because we do not dare that they are difficult.

— LUCIUS ANNAEUS SENECA

High in the French Alps, at a sidewalk café on a cobbled street in the
ski town of Bourg-Saint-Maurice, two whitewater paddlers sat drinking beer and speculating about the future. There are no photos of that
informal encounter, but they would have been tanned, fit, and clad in
shorts, sandals, and national team warm-up jackets for Czechoslovakia
and Austria. Above the red Bohemian lion rampant on his jacket,
Czech Jiří Bobák's regular features and conservative haircut, neither
hippie long nor soldier buzz-cut, belied the audacity of his proposal.
It was August 1969, and as Jeff Slater, Mike Jones, and the rest of the
British "accidental expedition" struggled deep in the Inn River canyons
of Switzerland, the elite of the whitewater kayak and canoe world
were gathered on the Isère River for the biannual world championships of slalom and downriver racing. These two men, from perennial
powerhouse countries, were at the very center of that world, and never
before had the future of whitewater sports appeared so exciting.

When Lowell Thomas sent Steve Bradley to scout northern Pakistan for locations to film whitewater kayaking in 1956, it took Bradley no more than a day to report back that kayaking of that era had
neither the equipment nor the skills to take on the challenge of the
Himalayas. But the ensuing decade had seen remarkable change.
Specialized designs of molded fiberglass replaced wood-and-canvas

boats. World-championship races limited to a few Central European nations grew annually in participation and difficulty, then became intercontinental with the addition of American paddlers Dick Dratton and Carol Kane — overwhelmed but game — in 1957. In the Alps, Europeans, and most recently Brits, were applying the new boats and skills to ever more audacious river running.

And now the previously unthinkable had just turned the whitewater world upside down. It had been announced that the obscure young sport of whitewater slalom was to be included in the Munich Olympic Games in 1972. Like their European neighbors, West and East Germany were leaders in the sport and ambitious for its growth. West Germany had exercised its prerogative as host to include slalom as a demonstration event, and they would build an unprecedented artificial whitewater stadium in Augsburg to showcase it. Whitewater was going to *the* show! Paddlers would appear on the world stage alongside sports icons from TV screens and the covers of glossy magazines around the world.

That summer of 1969 the "five ring fever" was just beginning to sink in. Dreaming of representing their sport and country, racers reached deep and found an intensity they did not know was in them. Former champions came out of retirement. Coaches studied training methods of sports like swimming and track and field to coax their athletes to new levels. Boat designers chased rumors about the artificial course, trying to anticipate ideal hull shapes for the unknown turbulence.

This euphoria surged beyond slalom racing, beyond even the Olympics. Over the chilled beers at that café in Bourg-Saint-Maurice, the talk ranged widely to include once secret dreams that only now, with the sport's new legitimacy and emerging skill levels, could be openly admitted. Earlier that summer Austrian kayakers had claimed a record for high-altitude kayaking on tributaries of the Indus River at more than ninety-eighty hundred feet in the Hindu Kush mountain range. Had the time arrived to mount expeditions even higher in the Himalayas? For whitewater sports to follow in the icy steps of the legendary mountaineers Mallory, Shipton and Tilman, Hillary and Tenzing Norgay, Hertzog, Terray . . . ?

Jeff Slater and his British paddlers had not been alone in the late 1960s, chafing under onerous government travel restrictions. Locked behind the Iron Curtain, Eastern Europeans faced more than economic barriers. Travel to the West was forbidden, except for those with connections and able to claim state-sanctioned business. Even for those lucky few, it was almost impossible to obtain hard currency to spend beyond the Soviet bloc. Sport was highly regarded across the communist world, both as a healthy occupation for the population and as Cold War propaganda on the international scene. If they were in good standing with the communist authorities, qualified competitors, coaches, and trainers could travel to recognized international events, although usually together as teams and under the strict supervision of government minders.

Czech whitewater racers had powered their way to the very top ranks in the world, and in 1967 their country had proudly hosted the world championships. Yet by 1969, Czech paddlers shared the restlessness and political tension that had led to the widespread protests and brutal Soviet crackdown of 1968. Beginning in about 1965, a movement had emerged embracing a more liberal interpretation of communist rule. Hope and idealism soared as the party loosened its constraints. Cultural exchanges with the West were eagerly embraced in sport and in the arts. Not since the Hungarian insurrection in 1956 had the iron fist of Soviet communism been so challenged, and Moscow and sister Warsaw Pact rulers looked on with alarm.

In August 1968, just one year prior to that meeting in Bourg-Saint-Maurice, Soviet Red Army tanks had occupied Prague overnight, putting a sudden, violent end to the "Prague Spring" movement that had filled the streets for months and to the government and party elements who had condoned it. Czech citizens who had most eagerly embraced Western contact and influence were now the most suspect and most restricted.

Jiří Bobák, however, was not one of them, and his dreams lay east, not west. After those exciting 1969 world championships, he drove back to Ostrava, a gritty industrial town in the heartland of Czechoslovakia, with his head full of dreams bigger even than the Olympics. In a television interview thirty-five years later, he would recount the tale of his chance encounter at that café in Bourg-Saint-Maurice and of a gentlemen's agreement sealed over tall glasses of beer. Whichever nation, Czechoslovakia or Austria, did better in the world championships would have the first opportunity to mount a full-scale Himalayan expedition and chase the altitude record. When the Czechs prevailed on the Isère River, only Bobák and his Austrian counterpart knew at the time the full implications of that victory.

Soot-blackened Ostrava was far removed from the heady breezes of the Prague Spring and its intellectual center at ancient Charles University, and in that working-class factory town it was no secret that Jiří Bobák was a man who got things done. Even though he was not an elite paddler himself, whitewater competition was his passion. He was an organizer, a manager, and it was in that capacity that he had been part of the Czech team at the world championships. As he drove home, he was almost overwhelmed by the enormity of putting together the world's first major kayaking expedition to the Himalayas: the nearly impossible bureaucracy of obtaining Czechoslovak Canoeing Union and government sanction; the logistics of transporting a team, their boats and supplies, across the length of Asia; the difficulty and danger of the whitewater — completely unknown, but surely analogous to the frequently deadly challenges of mountaineering in the highest mountains on Earth.

Recruiting and training a team for such a long and dangerous expedition might be the easiest part. Excellent paddlers bypassed in the national team selections, and those running whitewater rivers but not racing, had long envied their mountaineering comrades who could obtain permits and support to carry the Czechoslovakian flag to the great ranges of the world. By the time he joined the smoky queue of idling diesel trucks at the fortified checkpoint on the Austrian frontier between West and East, Jiří Bobák had recalled the advice of Roman author Seneca. He was resolved to "dare," to challenge the highest mountain on Earth — Everest.

Jiří Bobák stood transfixed, large wet snowflakes plastering his hair and jacket, and watched three and a half years of dreaming, planning, training, and equipping toboggan down a ravine high in the Caucasus Mountains, dragging behind its snapped safety cable. Their trailer — its boxy sides proudly painted with the expedition logo and announcing their mission in Czech and English — contained seven months of supplies for the expedition. Their rations, camp equipment, and boating gear careened in eerie silence down the icy mountain road, smashed through a rudimentary guardrail, and tumbled down the precipitous embankment.

Bobák had spent fourteen months since that fateful meeting in the French Alps contending with seeming endless bureaucracy to obtain permission for the expedition from the Czech state, the Communist Party, and the canoeing union. Vladimír Klečka, skeptical at first, had become Jiří's first recruit and invaluable right-hand man. Only after their application had undergone twenty-seven drafts had they received the brief, prized letter from Prague: "With the propagation of Czechoslovak canoeing in mind, the board of the Czechoslovak Canoeing Union agrees with the course of the preparations. We wish you good luck with the future work on this grand plan." They were at last free to announce their ambitious plan to the newspaper and TV station in Ostrava, to seek sponsorship, and to recruit a full team, on which they were required to include Slovaks as well as Czechs to be truly representative of the nation.

The core paddling team would include both one-man kayaks and two-man whitewater canoes. In that era of swiftly evolving boats and technique, it was still an open question which was superior for running rivers. The lighter and smaller kayak was quicker and more nimble in tight maneuvers, while the somewhat longer and much heavier tandem boat had perhaps more power and momentum in pushing through bigger rapids.*

Slovak kayakers Jozef Mathias and Vojtěch Potočý enthusiastically joined Czech kayaker Vladimír Klečka and the Czech tandem canoe teams of Arnošt Dostál / Jiří Kolesa and Kurt Mužík / Čestmír Výtisk.

So began a meticulous backward-planning process. The year 1973 would be the sixtieth anniversary of the foundation of the Czechoslovakian Canoe Union, an auspicious time to celebrate on Mount Everest. April and May would be the best months, before summer monsoon rains. For an April 1 launch on the Dudh Kosi River, the advance scouting party and the main body should rendezvous on March 19 at an airfield in Luklu, Nepal. To reach Luklu, the main body should cross the Nepalese border on March 1 and begin trekking in with porters from road's end on March 8. And so on, each deadline calculated back to that receipt of authorization on October 7, 1970.

The quest for sponsorship entailed the same challenges faced by expeditions worldwide — but with a few Socialist People's Republic twists. A local meatpacking plant offered support with canned pork products. However, while the plant had facilities for slaughter, cooking, and canning, they did not have livestock. Bobák resignedly struck "canned meat" from his list of items to obtain and penciled in "pigs."

Their big breakthrough came when the massive national iron and steel works NHKG, located just south of Ostrava, adopted the expedition as its official sponsor and agreed to "loan" them a new Czech-manufactured, all-wheel-drive Tatra truck. Cash to configure a new truck cabin for the long overland journey was not to be had, nor for a large trailer to carry seven months of supplies. They had to find a

* By the mid-1970s this choice resolved itself in the world of river running, and while the tandem canoe remained a fixture in racing, its use soon faded on the more difficult rivers. Thus, in addition to being the first major expedition in the Himalayas with whitewater boats of any kind, the Czechoslovakians were likely the last to attempt a major whitewater expedition in tandem canoes anywhere.

workers' state solution. NHKG came up with a heated indoor workshop, welding equipment, and steel in abundance. For nine months, team members devoted weekends to the construction of a sturdy boxlike trailer for supplies and a cleverly designed truck body with kitchenette, crew seating, lockers, and sleeping modules.

As the British had done on the Inn River with Bonington and his friends, the Czechs included skilled climbers in their team for extra access and rescue. Taking advantage of their two-year lead time, the paddlers also trained in basic mountaineering skills, culminating in a team climb of Mont Blanc, the highest peak in Europe.

Confident in their preparation but aware of all the unknowns they faced, "The First Czechoslovakian Expedition to the Himalayas" rolled out of smoggy Ostrava on January 4, 1973. In addition to the Tatra truck and equipment trailer, their entourage included a GAZ (a jeeplike Romanian off-road vehicle) towing a light trailer carrying their boats. The sixteen-man team almost outnumbered the few relatives and friends gathered in a barren lot on the outskirts of town to see them off. *That will be different on our return*, they had vowed to themselves.

And now this, not yet halfway to Mount Everest. It was not just that their personal dreams and years of preparation were plunging out of control down a mountainside in the Caucasus; they also felt the weight of responsibility to one another as a team, to their sport, and as official representatives of their nation. Any thought of failure was particularly galling because the normally strong Czech national team paddlers had performed below expectations at the Munich Olympics the previous year. For some, to celebrate the sixtieth anniversary of the Czechoslovak Canoe Union on Mount Everest, natural whitewater, rather than the man-made concrete of Augsburg, would mean redemption; to fail would further wound their pride.

Struggling to keep their footing in the snow and ice, the stunned team worked their way to where the runaway trailer had come to an abrupt halt, pinned by trees and snow on the precipitous downhill slope, its frame grotesquely twisted and its sheet-metal sides sprung open like some monstrous, industrial flower. Dismay turned quickly to relief. Inside the wreck, miraculously, their tons of irreplaceable supplies were unscathed. They could only conclude that the cargo was packed in so tightly that it had rumbled downslope like one solid, massive boulder, crushing guardrails and underbrush, even as the trailer frame itself finally ripped open from its impact with the trees. Their conditioning on Mont Blanc now served them well, as they carried all the supplies by hand back up the steep slope to the road. They would now reconstruct the mangled trailer they had built themselves in a tiny workshop high in the Caucasus Mountains. Jiří Bobák had allowed for the unplanned. They were still on their timeline.

The Czechoslovakian team had practiced their river skills with particular intensity for the last three years leading up to the expedition. They had trained for mountaineering on Mont Blanc. And, reluctantly, they had honed their bureaucratic skills as well while obtaining travel permits and resources. As they drove up to the border crossing from India into Nepal, the final leg of their two-month overland trek, they were about to discover that the bureaucracy bequeathed upon South Asia by the British Raj was, if anything, even more stultifying than that of the communist states.

Warily eyeing their huge box trailer, and the boat trailer behind the GAZ with its torpedo-shaped fiberglass boats — so different from any Everest expedition equipment ever seen before — Nepalese customs officials demanded itemized lists of all their equipment and supplies. Each discrete item, whether hardware, clothing, or packages of food, was to be identified, with values, dimensions, and weight specified, and listed by whether it was to be consumed in Nepal or reexported at the conclusion of the expedition. Lists and dimensions would only be accepted in English. Values only in dollars. No exceptions for cans of donated pork sausages.

Warned by previous climbing expeditions, Jiří Bobák and his team came prepared. Their retinue included individuals with medical, mechanical, welding, cooking, and photography skills. And a rescue team member, Oldřich Vašek, spoke English. For months, team secretary and jack-of-all-trades Vladimír Klečka had labored over detailed, hand-drawn spreadsheets of foodstuffs; rescue climber Jirka Tomčala had done likewise for other supplies and equipment; and Oldřich had rendered both documents into the English required by the minions of the king in Kathmandu. The frontier barrier rose before the GAZ and its trailer full of whitewater boats, the lumbering Tatra truck, its fabricated crew cabin, and its rebuilt cargo trailer.

April 2, 1973, dawned bright and cold in Pheriche, high on the flanks of Mount Everest. Giving the sun time to clear the mountain ridges and begin to thaw the frozen valley, the Czechoslovakian team carried their boats and gear down to the river and meticulously recorded: altitude 4,243 meters (13,921 feet), air 9 degrees Celsius (48.2 Fahrenheit), water 4.7 degrees Celsius (40.5 Fahrenheit). A paddle jammed into a crack in a cliff face suspended a Czechoslovakian flag above the water to mark the occasion. The first paddlers launched downstream.

They knew that big rapids, falls, and difficult climbs lay ahead, but well downstream, and not this day. Their put-in was absolutely as far upstream as could be navigated in a whitewater boat, and the Dudh Kosi, which thundered downstream, was here barely a creek, a trout stream. On a paddling weekend in their home Tatra Mountains, they would not have considered running such insignificant riffles. The one-man kayaks barely managed to scrape down the narrow channels, the only casualty a wooden paddle wedged and cracked in the shallow rocks. The larger two-man canoes could not even do that; their teams were forced to abandon the attempt and put in again farther downstream. No matter. They were paddlers, and finally they were back in their boats after the grueling road and foot march. The

First Czechoslovakian Expedition to the Himalayas was no longer a dream, a dare, a five-year plan. It was real. Whatever happened from this point on, they had made history.

Side streams, milk white from glacial scour, poured in from the surrounding mountains. On the third morning the tandem canoes rejoined as mile by mile the Dudh Kosi grew from shallow rock gardens to exhilarating, nearly continuous rapids. The boaters progressed cautiously downstream, eddy-hopping and waiting as the support team on the bank scouted ahead and set rescue. This was to be their procedure wherever possible, and Jiří Bobák's plans called for only two or three miles each day. Success in representing their country, and especially the Czechoslovak Canoeing Union, would be determined in equal measure by running as much of the river as possible and doing so with appropriate safety and sportsmanship.

An inaccessible canyon, with vertical walls that would make rescue impossible and, from the little they could see, rapids that were very difficult, if not impossible, forced them away from the river entirely. In a snowstorm, porters carried the boats down through the narrow teeming streets of the Sherpa "capital," Namche Bazar, to a point where they could resume their descent.

Kurt Mužík stood frozen on a narrow ledge, the river churning below, endless rock above, able neither to climb upward nor to back down. His fatigued calf muscles beat a sewing machine rhythm, and his aching hands and forearms threatened to lose their grip at any moment. He desperately wanted to scream for help, but even his voice seemed paralyzed. Sometimes the careful scouting ahead on land was as risky as the rapids. His teammates finally saw his predicament from above, dropped him a rope, and lowered him to the relative safety of the river. The mountaineering training had been useful, but he was, after all, a paddler, not a climber.

The river now was bigger, pushier, more continuous — the most

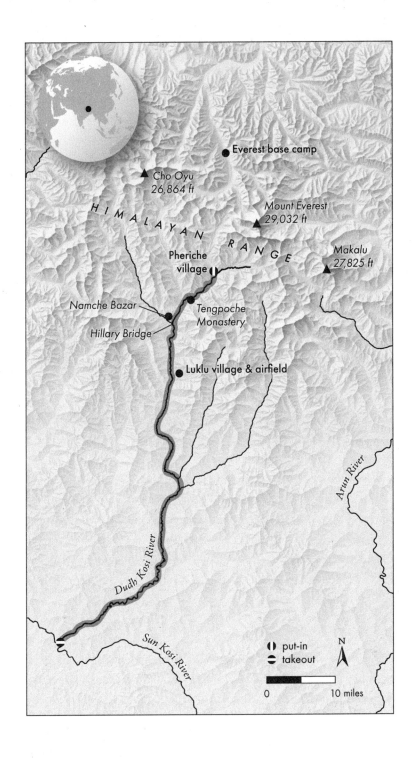

Everest base camp

Cho Oyu
26,864 ft

HIMALAYAN

Mount Everest
29,032 ft

RANGE

Makalu
27,825 ft

Pheriche
village

Namche Bazar

Tengpoche
Monastery

Hillary Bridge

Luklu village & airfield

Arun River

Dudh Kosi River

Sun Kosi River

◖ put-in
◗ takeout

N

0   10 miles

difficult conditions any of them had ever paddled. The greatest adventure of their lives. Six hundred cubic feet of water, forty-two degrees cold, flowed downstream through the Dudh Kosi's boulder-choked bed each second. The safety teams on shore frequently had to assist the boaters in stopping. Recirculating holes formed below every drop, and the boats could only punch through the big ones at their corners. Youngest of the paddlers at twenty-five, Jozef Mathias maneuvered his kayak through a series of waves and chutes, then hit a hole wrong and flipped. He rolled up quickly, only to capsize in another hole before he could regain control. His paddle blade hit a rock on the next attempt as he was swept past the first pair of rescuers, toward a potentially deadly drop ahead. He surfaced, swimming, barely in time to reach the outstretched hands of the last safety team.

Cautioned by Jozef's misadventure, the other boaters made it through the section with one Eskimo roll but no further swims. As they regrouped to proceed, they were alerted by shouts and cheers from the Sherpas upstream. Jozef, who had carried back up the bank, appeared, paddling stronger, determined to salvage his pride and to run that section in proper style. As he pulled into the final eddy, his teammates joined the Sherpas in applauding him for his nerve and tenacity. It was his proudest moment.

One stretch of the river was bound on both sides by vertical rim walls, choking off all view, and all possibility of entry on foot for scouting or rescue. To attempt running it without knowledge of what lay within would be madness, however, so the veteran mountaineers included in the expedition team deployed a winch-and-rope system to lower a harnessed scout six hundred vertical feet to check out the river. It was runnable!

Early in their planning, Bobák and Klečka had studied, almost in disbelief, the histories of expeditions in the Himalayas and elsewhere that had gone spectacularly wrong. Teams of elite climbers totally breaking apart, leaving their companions in peril. Experienced seamen abandoning their ships. Even murder and suicide in the desert wastes. Now, just as the team's nerve, paddling skills, and climbing skills were being tested to their limits, so too were their health and morale. Vladimír Klečka had been suffering from a pulmonary infection since they first arrived at altitude; he had been forced to spend much of the expedition in shore support, not paddling. Čestmír Výtisk wrenched his back in an awkward stumble as he and his partner, Kurt Mužík, carried their tandem canoe on the boulder-strewn bank. Hours each night, and sometimes full days, were devoted to healing their injured bodies and broken fiberglass boats.

Their canned sausages, those hard-won pigs, had deteriorated and were only palatable with massive doses of mustard. The bread was beyond hard, and other food was spoiled completely. Their alternatives were local foods almost certain to promote dysentery or worse. Any given day half a dozen or more would be suffering from gastrointestinal distress, and double doses of medication had little more than a placebo effect. Already skinny, Jiří Kolesa dropped almost eighteen pounds before reaching home. Of them all, their non-paddling leader, Jiří Bobák, lost the most: thirty-five pounds. Only expedition doctor Miroslav Rozehnal, age sixty-four, a Nazi concentration camp survivor and old Asia hand, would make it to the end without illness or injury of one sort or anotl 2r.

Their extended time away from home, and the lack of privacy in the truck cabin and crowded tent camps, exacerbated real stress and petty annoyance alike. The climbers had come along to support scouting and rescue for the descent team but also hoping to scale a minor Himalayan peak themselves. Time free from river team obligations was limited, however, and their brief attempt was weathered out. Resentment festered; harsh words were exchanged. Hunger, illness, and dissatisfaction with the food flared out against the cook personally — almost a cliché, from cattle roundup and mining camp to modern expedition. Choices made on the river erupted from discussions to stormy arguments. The accounts Bobák had studied of major conflagrations that had broken apart previous expeditions began to take on foreboding relevance.

Vladimír Klečka recorded, "We've improved a lot since coming here. Our lungs should have increased capacity and our blood should be adapted to the lack of oxygen. Our hearts should be large enough to need half the beats of a normal person to do its job. But our job wasn't just to find large and efficient hearts but also hearts that are capable of understanding and working in a team." With Jiří Bobák's steady leadership and Dr. Miroslav Rozehnal's infectious optimism and stamina, they maintained their focus on their common goal. Wounds healed, petty arguments resolved, and the broken boats were repaired each night.

And the Dudh Kosi relented. Day by day, the mountain walls pulled back, jungle replaced sheer rock, tiny hamlets appeared in clearings high above. The river had swollen to a thousand cubic feet per second and more, but its bed became wider and less steep. Huge waves and holes were easier to avoid, while big eddies and pools between the rapids made rescue much more certain. The first monsoon rains began to fall. It was April 21, and they were still in compliance with the master timeline.

Jiří Bobák, the non-paddling promoter and master organizer, stepped into the bow of Arnošt Dostál's tandem canoe, sealed his sprayskirt around the cockpit rim, and gave one last tug to the chinstrap of his helmet. The pair stroked awkwardly into the current, narrowly avoiding a series of rocks. The current quickened, and downstream the river funneled into a train of six-foot exploding waves. Perched in the very front of the fifteen-foot boat, Jiří gulped for air each time the bow rose up the face of a wave, seeming to thrust him into the sky, then grimaced as the boat teeter-tottered on the crest and plunged him deep into the trough below. He had finally run a rapid in the Himalayas, and he was deeply content. Just downstream, the Dudh Kosi ended its race down

Mount Everest at the golden sands of the Sun Kosi River. Together, the Czechoslovakian paddlers had shown the world how to mount a whitewater canoe and kayak expedition halfway around the world, how to safely run a river in the highest mountains on the planet. How to dare.

CHAPTER FOUR

Mother of Rivers

The Kali Gandaki River

> And from this chasm, with ceaseless turmoil seething,
> As if this earth in fast thick pants were breathing,
> A mighty fountain momently was forced.
>
> — SAMUEL TAYLOR COLERIDGE, *Kubla Khan*

Hans Memminger, one of West Germany's foremost kayakers, watched
the thrilling preparations for the 1972 Olympics and plans to build the
artificial whitewater course in Augsburg from Rosenheim, a town just
thirty miles outside Munich. A former racer, now river runner and
filmmaker with piercing eyes and an unselfconscious gap-toothed grin,
he, like Jiří Bobák, saw the Olympics as a springboard to that secret
dream: the Himalayas. But where the Czechs would reach for altitude,
toward the gleaming ice peaks of the Himalayan gods, Memminger
was drawn to the depths, to somber gorges where the bright sky is
censored by rock and where Earth's irresistible tectonic and geomor-
phic processes collide in earthquake and flood. Nowhere did that
relentless drama unfold as on the Kali Gandaki River in central Nepal.

During the Upper Cretaceous period, near the end of the dinosaur
age, the Indian continental plate slammed into and under the Eurasian
plate, beginning to raise the Tibetan Plateau to become "the roof of the
world." It forced the bed of the Tethyan Sea skyward in a massive
tectonic uplift that continues today, forming the fifteen-hundred-mile
arc of the Himalayan mountains — the youngest and tallest range on
the planet. Like a titanic dam, it forces the mightiest rivers of Asia to
flow around its ends in their imperative to seek the sea. From headwaters near sacred Mount Kailash in western Tibet, the Indus flows

west-northwest, parallel to the mountain barrier, until it breaks south
around Nanga Parbat, the western anchor of the Himalayas, where Bus
Hatch and Otto Lang encountered it in 1956. Also, from headwaters near
Mount Kailash, the Tsangpo flows the length of the mountain range to
the east-northeast, looping in a mysterious gorge around the Himalayas'
eastern terminus, Mount Namcha Barwa, to emerge as the Brahmaputra
on the Indian Plain. Equally cut off from southern flow, the third longest
river in the world, the Yangtze, plunges east to nurture teeming China.

Yet not all rivers respect that vast tectonic barrier. In central Nepal, at
what might be described as the midpoint of the great arc of the Himalayas, the Kali Gandaki ("Kali's river" in Sanskrit) cleaves the mountain
range in two. More ancient than the mountains, sacred to a billion and
a half Hindu worshippers, this antecedent river has gnawed the mountain roots for seventy million years. Like a divine saw powered by gravity and time, lubricated by the torrential rains of the Indian monsoon,
and toothed with tons of rock and grit rendered from the mountains
themselves by glaciers, she cuts her ancient course all the way from Tibet
to India. Between sister giants Annapurna and Dhaulagiri, whose icy
peaks loom more than twenty-six thousand feet in the sky, her eighteen-
thousand-foot-deep abyss drew Memminger like a dark siren.*

Memminger and his two companions drifted in swift current beneath
a chain bridge festooned with colorful prayer flags and lined with curious Nepalese observers. Although the icy mountaintops were hidden
behind steep shoulders of vegetation and rock outcrops that seemed
to rise forever, he could feel the weight, the invisible presence of the
immense massifs on either hand. He had little time to contemplate the
grandeur above, however. Almost immediately the banks steepened,
constraining the writhing current in its narrowed bed, and ahead the
horizon line of a major drop sent them scrambling for the safety of

*Mount Dhaulagiri (26,795 feet) and Mount Annapurna (26,545 feet) stand twenty-
four miles apart, and in the chasm directly between, the Kali Gandaki flows at 8,270
feet — an awesome depth of 18,278 feet.

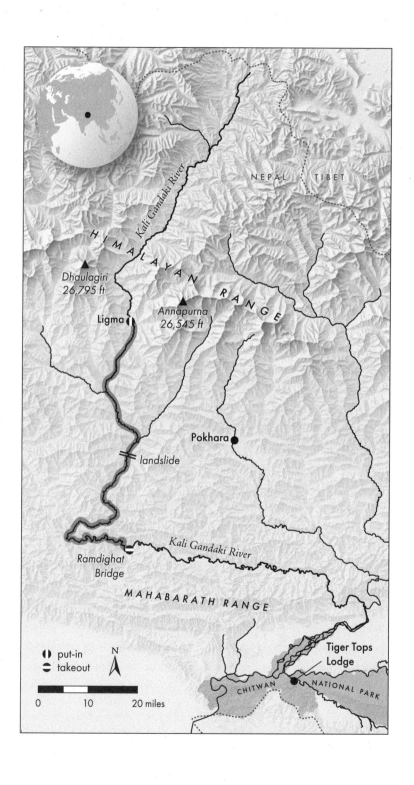

NEPAL · TIBET

Kali Gandaki River

H I M A L A Y A N   R A N G E

Dhaulagiri
26,795 ft

Ligma

Annapurna
26,545 ft

Pokhara

landslide

Kali Gandaki River

Ramdighat
Bridge

M A H A B A R A T H   R A N G E

put-in
takeout

N

0   10   20 miles

Tiger Tops
Lodge

CHITWAN · NATIONAL PARK

shoreline eddies. Memminger could feel the sluggish weight of expedition gear inside his kayak, so unlike the joyful play with empty boats
that they had experienced earlier during warm-up runs on more accessible rivers. It changed his timing and balance, and it would take some
time and miles for his muscle memory to adapt.

In their spartan bivouac that night, masses of rock loomed above
the three kayakers as inconceivable and unknown as the hazards below.
Would they find gradients too steep, flows too powerful for their skills?
Landslides that blocked the narrow canyon completely? Unclimbable
cliffs on both sides of the river? No roads or known trails allowed views
into this gorge, nor had they been able to overfly their route. They knew
only that their objective, a road at Ramdighat, lay ninety-three miles
downstream and thirty-six hundred feet below. They were now fully
committed, and from downstream the abyss stared back at them.

They were also now utterly alone. Hans Memminger, kayaker and
rafter Fred Schmidtkonz, and kayaker and veteran Himalayan and
Alaskan climber Otto Huber had no train of porters carrying supplies
and setting camps, no mountaineers in overwatch, no extra boats,
and no communication with the outside world. The three quickly
fell into a smooth camp routine: Schmidtkonz saw to the fire and
cooking, Huber measured elevations and plotted their progress, and
Memminger recorded everything on film.

They would be self-supported until they emerged at the other end. In
mountaineering parlance, this was Alpine style. Everything they would
need they must find within themselves and their now eighty-eight-pound
kayaks. Aware that their lives depended on maneuvering (and Eskimo
rolling) in extremely difficult water, and mindful of every ounce weighing
them down, they had pared their kit to sleeping bags; six days of rations
and medications; 260 feet of climbing rope, along with hammer, pitons,
ascenders, and carabiners; and a 16mm film camera, still camera, and film.
All was sealed in waterproof bags in the ends of the thirteen-foot boats.[*]

---

[*] In this early era of fiberglass whitewater kayaks, the models used for running rivers
were those designed for slalom racing; more specialized adaptations had not yet evolved.
And by the arbitrary rules of racing, those kayaks were four meters in length (roughly
thirteen feet).

For thirty miles the Kali Gandaki offered no respite. Too steep for the men to see more than about one hundred feet ahead from their boats, it tore downstream in chutes between massive boulders dislodged from steep gorge walls, presented only minuscule eddies in which to stop, and formed violent, recirculating holes. Barely managing to punch through one such stopper, Memminger was plunged immediately into another. Helpless without momentum, his boat swung sideways and was trapped against the wall of whitewater crashing back upstream into the hole, like breaking surf on a stormy ocean. Bracing on a paddle blade sunk into the turbulence, he balanced as his hull skipped violently up and down on the swift current flowing into the hole from upstream, but with all his strength he was unable to force the kayak out of the hole. Soon all his arm strength would be spent.

Fighting the forces of nature at this scale was futile. He must use them — dance with them. Gasping as much air into his lungs as he could, he deliberately relaxed his braced paddle, letting the water grab his upstream gunwale and capsize him into the maelstrom. And then he waited, fighting the urge to Eskimo roll upright, into the precious air. Doing so too soon would simply return him to the trap. Hanging his body and paddle as deep as possible like a sea anchor in the current flowing downstream beneath the recirculating hole, he waited. Suddenly he felt an eerie quiet, his kayak no longer bucking in the chaos of the hole. He was washing downstream, at current speed. Hastily he curled his body forward against the deck, rolled the boat upright, and powered forward even as he shook the water from his eyes to look for the next obstacle.

From the vibrant heart of Western Europe in 1974, Memminger and his companions had faced none of the bureaucratic obstacles encountered by the Czechs the previous year in the Eastern sector. They required no official sanction to travel abroad, no support or equipment from state enterprises, no ethnic balancing to represent their country. But without state backing, they still needed funds and equipment, as well as permission and cooperation from Nepal. The answer, and their second objective, was the brainchild of fellow Bavarian Günter Hauser, a climber and founder of trekking and adventure travel company Hauser Exkursionen International who also served as the honorary consul for Nepal in Munich. Before and after their Kali Gandaki adventure, they were to scout easier and more accessible rivers suitable to launch the first whitewater tourism in Nepal. West German boat and sporting equipment manufacturers, as well as the government of Nepal, where mountaineering and trekking were the major source of foreign income, jumped eagerly aboard.

With a team of just three men, they had even arranged to fly to Kathmandu, avoiding the time and logistical problems of overland travel from Europe. One day they had been in Bavaria, sorting gear, making last-minute plans. The next, they strained to see, through the aircraft windows, one of the grandest panoramas on the planet. Only climber Otto Huber had been to Nepal before, and he pointed out the legendary peaks: in the east, Kanchenjunga and Makalu, then Everest, Langtang, and, irresistibly drawing their eyes farther west, Annapurna and Dhaulagiri. The ice wall gleaming in the sun seemed to stretch unbroken across the horizon. Both awe and tension filled the aircraft cabin as it sank in that they would soon be thousands of feet deep within those mountains, attempting rivers no man had run before.

In front of the three dismayed paddlers, one of their worst fears materialized. As if finally defeated in the vise grip of the mountains, the Kali Gandaki vanished, consumed by a massive rockslide that filled the gorge as far as they could see. The rush and grumble of the rapids that reverberated off the mountain walls, which had become their constant companion day and night, was silent. Cautiously they picked their way through the last shallow patches of water and clambered on foot onto a vast field of house-sized boulders. Burning sun, exhausting heat, and searing thirst replaced icy swift water as they struggled between and over the broken rocks with their gear-laden kayaks, until that too became impossible. Negotiating a nine-hundred-foot sheer cliff was unavoidable.

Now the climbing gear that had been their burden became their salvation. As they worked their way upward, they could see scarring and water marks on the canyon walls a hundred feet above the present floor, reminders that the Kali Gandaki was not, after all, defeated by the mountains — only resting for her next monsoon-force assault.

From the height, shining glimpses of the river appeared down the canyon, only to disappear again beneath more rockfall. Several back-breaking hours had passed, and they had barely progressed down-stream. But teeming, tumultuous Asia is not the sweeping far-northern wilderness of North America or Siberia. Even the most remote spots are inhabited, and the more remote the spot, it seems, the more curious are the inhabitants. Along invisible trails, drawn by mysterious intelligence, Nepalese appeared, silently observing. Sign language and rupees enlisted willing allies, and the expedition was, briefly at least, no longer pure Alpine style. Eager hands lifted the boats and led the way five hundred yards down the canyon, to a spot where the Kali Gandaki emerged from its imprisonment and again appeared navigable.

Except sheer rock dropped straight into the river's flow, without the slightest tiny beach or ledge on which to get into their boats. Of necessity, they slid into their boats and sealed their spray decks while balanced on a ledge above, tipped forward, and plunged down the rock face into the water below, in what Memminger dubbed a Himalaya-start.*

On the third day, with about thirty miles behind them, the difficulty of the rapids had not diminished, but, almost imperceptibly at first, then distinctly, the three paddlers could feel them becoming more spaced out. Eddies were larger, and there were pools below some drops. Another landslide choked off the gorge, but they carried over it with now-practiced ease. Huts appeared in tiny clearings high on the hillsides. Their tension

---

* Now commonly called a seal launch, this has become, since the advent of tough, roto-molded plastic kayaks, a common technique even among beginners. Although known to Memminger and his teammates, it was much less common in the era of more fragile fiberglass.

eased as their safety margins increased, and Memminger could write, "Day after day the Kali-Gandaki sang his wild melody to us, we took his sounds with us to sleep, he became like a trusted friend to us."

Five days after they threw themselves into the Kali Gandaki Gorge, now ninety-three miles downstream, thirty-six hundred feet below, and each man ten to twelve pounds lighter, they shouldered their laden boats for the final time and, with a mixture of relief and regret, climbed the riverbank to a waiting jeep at Ramdighat. It was time to complete their second objective.

Before tackling the Kali Gandaki, they had run three other untried river sections in Nepal, warm-ups before their major challenge as well as scouting for river touring opportunities for Günter Hauser and his partner in Nepal, Rinchen Lama. Two days on the Trisuli River, not far north of Kathmandu, revealed a beautiful valley, a medium flow of surprisingly warm water (relative to the Alps they were used to), and a drop-pool pattern of rapids of moderate difficulty. "Conclusion — an interesting wild river, ideal for guided tours," read Memminger's final report. Next came the Marsyangdi River, on the eastern flanks of Annapurna, its exotic banks set with white-flowering magnolia and colorful birds. Troops of monkeys added to the now-familiar crowds of villagers who followed their every move. The river squeezed into a small gorge, delighting the three kayakers with its steep rapids and warm water. "Short of nothing to please the kayaker."

While staging in Pokhara to trek to the Kali Gandaki, they had also elected to take a final warm-up run on the nearby Seti-Khola River. Deep within its narrow gorge, the milky-green glacial river disappeared underground — not even a gurgle — and almost took them with it. It was after dark before they could extract themselves from the labyrinth of rock and water to find their vehicle and driver. No river for the commercial market, and hardly providing the rest day they had anticipated, the Seti-Khola was, perhaps, a caution against overconfidence when they launched down the Kali Gandaki.

Now with their great adventure completed, Memminger, Huber, and Schmidtkonz loaded their boats onto the vehicle and drove downstream to complete their reconnaissance for Günter Hauser and his dream of commercial rafting in Nepal. Between the mountain peaks and highlands of the Himalayan massif and the Terai, the tropical wetlands teeming with all the jungle fauna of the Indian Plain, lie the forest-shrouded Mahabarath Mountains. Once again self-supported, the kayakers launched into the gorge cut by the Kali Gandaki through this nine-thousand-foot barrier, less worried about the rapids ahead than about the tigers, crocodiles, and rhinoceroses whose world they would be entering.

Occasional easy rapids enlivened their otherwise swift float through a wild and pristine cross section of South Asia. The monsoon was coming on, bright flashing lightning illuminated dripping, mossy canyon walls, and screaming troops of monkeys and exotic waterfowl met them at every bend. Fittingly, their run ended at Tiger Tops, the world-famous wildlife observation lodge at the core of Nepal's first national park, Chitwan. To add to their list of firsts (and to adorn Günter Hauser's promotional literature), they persuaded Tiger Tops to shuttle them and their boats out of the jungle to the nearest roadhead on the backs of elephants normally used to safely observe tigers in the wild.*

In November of that same year, Hauser Exkursionen International launched the first commercial tour group of fifteen kayakers down the lower Kali Gandaki to Tiger Tops. Over the next several years Hans Memminger returned to Nepal time and again, training young Nepalese as raft guides to fulfill Günter Hauser's and Rinchen Lama's dream of developing river tourism as a source of employment and a robust part of the Nepalese economy, on a par with trekking and mountaineering.

* Memminger and his team were the first to kayak this route. They were not, however, the first to navigate it. In 1972, French anthropologist and explorer Michel Peissel buzzed both up and down this stretch in a small hovercraft, in a quirky attempt to prove hovercraft a practical means of transport on rivers in roadless regions. Peissel wisely did not attempt the great gorge upstream.

CHAPTER FIVE

A Meteoric Decade

The Dudh Kosi, Orinoco, and Braldu Rivers

Mike Jones was the instigator and inspiration of a small
group of Britons who led the world in expedition canoeing.
— SIR CHRIS BONINGTON

Down the Kathmandu Trail blazed by thousands of 1960s hippies,
Mike Jones launched his next international expedition in the summer
of 1976. Over the mountain passes of Turkey, across the vast plains of
Iran and deserts of Afghanistan, through flooded roads in the Indian
foothills, the six-member team drove, broke down, improvised repairs,
and negotiated their way across international borders. If the romance
of Africa, crocodiles, and bandits had not been enough to capture the
attention of sponsors and a popular audience, they would go where
British climbers, and notably Chris Bonington, were achieving fame.
They would kayak down Mount Everest! And for good measure,
they would set a Guinness World Record for kayaking at altitude by
paddling from the source of the Dudh Kosi River, near the Everest
base camp!

The paddlers, who were known to one another, skilled at their
roles, and unified in their goals, bonded even more tightly throughout
the long road march. Joining Mike were Mick Hopkinson, his friend
and partner on the Upper Blue Nile; John Liddell, who had paddled
the Grand Canyon with Mike; and Robert Hastings, known to them
all from the slalom circuit, where he had been a member of the British team since age sixteen. Rounding out the lineup, based on their

good chemistry with Mike, were Roger Huyton and the young Dave Manby, who was less experienced than Mike himself had been on the Inn in 1969. Due in part to an entire double floor of their Bedford van consisting of cases of Turkish beer for crossing the parched deserts of Iran and Afghanistan, the team made the rugged six-week journey without a single argument or falling-out, proudly commemorating their mileage each day on the van walls with Magic Marker, and forging a comradery that would last not only down the Dudh Kosi but also for their lifetimes.

The Czechs in 1973 and the Germans in 1974 had shown the way for those dedicated few within whitewater sports, but neither had succeeded in placing kayaking on the same plane in the public imagination as mountaineering in the Himalayas. Maybe that required more showmanship. Mike would no longer rely on his single, hand-held 16mm Bolex for media coverage, shooting as he had time among all his other expedition activities. Rather, the expedition was designed to prioritize the production of a first-class film. Mike had teamed up early on with Leo Dickinson, a highly regarded mountaineering and adventure filmmaker, and together the two had organized their team of thirteen Brits: six paddlers, two cameramen with two support climbers, and three in logistical support.

Expedition kayaking in the Himalayas requires additional skills to those for racing or day-tripping, even on the most difficult Alpine rivers. The Czechs had trained by climbing Mont Blanc. The Brits trained by swimming the Eiskanal, the artificial whitewater course built in Augsburg for the 1972 Olympics. Its molded concrete had no cracks or sharp edges to entrap or severely injure a swimmer, yet its currents were even faster and more chaotic than a natural stream-bed. German slalom racers, who struggled to stay upright and avoid swimming from their boats, were bemused by the Brits as they flushed through the run from top to bottom, hundreds of repetitions, with life jackets and without. Their aim was to synchronize their gasping breath with their irregular pulsations to the surface until doing so became rote muscle memory, instinctive. Their preparation would later prove lifesaving.

Mike glibly estimated the adventure would be a three-month excursion overall. As it unfolded, those who knew him best noted that one thing had not changed: Rupert's planning anticipated green lights all along the way. Yet before they even reached the put-in, more than two of those three months had already elapsed: three weeks training in Austria and Germany, four weeks driving overland, and two more weeks trekking in.

Mike's plans also called for all rivers to be swollen. Today's technology of rotomolded, nearly indestructible polyethylene kayaks was still in the embryonic stages and not yet a practical option. On the Inn he had seen the daily attrition as their fiberglass and polyester resin boats were smashed beyond repair in the steep, rock-choked Alpine drops, until only he and Dave Allen had the equipment to complete the run. His experience on the Colorado was just the opposite. The rigid eggshell kayaks withstood the rock-free but immensely larger and more powerful water of the Grand Canyon relatively well. There were big pools, often miles of flat water, between the big rapids, and so long as the paddler had an excellent roll below the rapids, all went well.

Likely because of these two formative experiences, he sought high water as he planned expeditions for the rest of his life. On the Blue Nile, he and Mick Hopkinson had plunged into the upper gorge at the tail end of the monsoon season. They quickly concluded, rightly or wrongly, that in the boiling, tightly constricted channel a swimmer would have no chance of rescue or survival, which led to their wedging themselves into their boats with their equipment. The Eskimo roll was to be their only rescue. That approach had worked on the Blue Nile, so, undeterred, Mike planned his run down the flanks of Mount Everest during the height of the Indian monsoon.

As always, Chris Bonington was supportive: "Yes, I think it will go. Although it does look bloody difficult. It must rank in canoeing terms the same as climbing Everest — the dangers are about the same." He

provided Mike and his team with films of the river shot during his
1975 approach march to climb the Southwest Ridge of Everest, which
were simultaneously helpful and, due to a lack of scale, deceptive.

Other pundits were less sanguine. Evidently unaware of the Czech
run in 1973, the executive director of outfitter Mountain Travel in
Kathmandu wrote, "Not really our concern, but, in spite of Chris
Bonington's & Peter Steel's remarks, we have some considerable
doubts as to the feasibility of your plan. Our combined Mountain
Travel expertise is considerably greater than Bonington & Steel's.
Frankly we do not think you can canoe down from Pheriche to junc-
tion of Sunkosi . . ." Mountain Travel, however, did provide logistic
support — paid in advance.

The overland drive out to Nepal had taken weeks more than
Rupert's optimistic ten-day estimate. He feared they would lose the
monsoon spate he wanted on the river; most team members had lives
and obligations to return to in England; and each day, porter fees
drained their limited coffers. Determined to lose no more time, and to
achieve their objectives, Mike had split the party at the wooden bridge
at Pheriche, where the Czechs had previously launched.

Mike and Mick hastened toward the Khumbu Glacier in pursuit of
the high-altitude world record for kayaking. At the end of their trek
in, his eyes in searing pain from snow blindness, Mike could barely
see to follow Mick's silhouette as the two stumbled, kayaks on their
shoulders, lungs gasping in the thin air, over jumbles of snow and
rock to the ice-choked lake below the Everest base camp. Chunks of
broken ice many times the size of their kayaks ground together across
the surface. Fresh icebergs calved off the nose of the Khumbu Glacier
with cracks like cannon fire, launching sheets of icy spray and roiling
the icy surface. Under attentive camera lenses, the pair launched and
inched their way through channels of bobbling ice chunks, trying to
avoid the crumbling glacier wall and the largest icebergs.

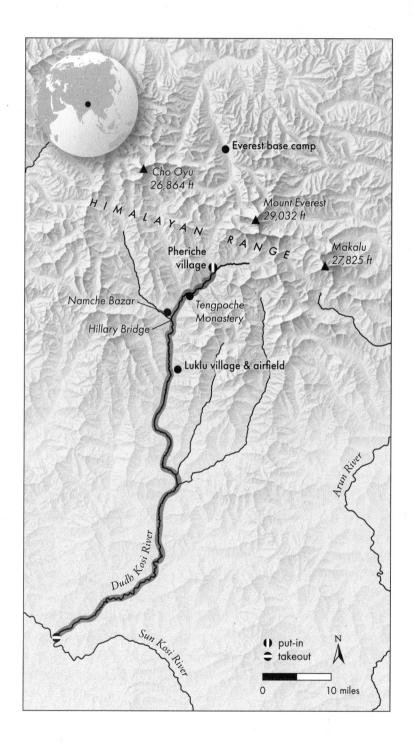

Everest base camp

Cho Oyu
26,864 ft

HIMALAYAN
RANGE

Mount Everest
29,032 ft

Makalu
27,825 ft

Pheriche
village

Namche Bazar

Tengpoche
Monastery

Hillary Bridge

Luklu village & airfield

Arun River

Dudh Kosi River

Sun Kosi River

() put-in
⊖ takeout

N

0   10 miles

At the end of the lake, any hopes they might have had of continuing down the streambed of the Dudh Kosi from its very start were dashed. Water seeped from the lake in tiny rivulets that alternately appeared and disappeared into a gigantic scree slope, and no coherent stream seemed likely for miles. The light was red. With their world record of kayaking (although not whitewater) at 17,500 feet in the can, they hastened down to rejoin the main body of the expedition.

The remaining paddlers began their descent on September 15. Initially the Dudh Kosi was small — just twenty feet wide, shallow, and boulder-choked. Rocks snatched at their paddles, capsizes were punishing even with their helmets and padded life jackets, and there was constant risk of pinning sideways in the congested channels. The "rock gardens" were more continuous than they were accustomed to; eddies were few in which to rest their oxygen-starved lungs at 14,300 feet. Shivering from the glacial water, but grateful for the recovery time, the paddlers waited wherever they could for the signal that Leo Dickinson and his cameras were repositioned downstream to record their descent, just as Mike and the British team had done for Bonington on the Inn River years before.

The river became wider and more powerful, but its rapids no less continuous. Dave Manby became the first to experience the wrath of the Himalayan torrent, pulled to shore blue-lipped, hypothermic, and almost insensate by Rob Hastings after a missed roll and a violent hundred-yard swim. Dave's mangled boat was claimed by the porters and became the expedition's first sacrifice to the mountain gods: a fiberglass henhouse at the storied Tengboche Monastery, where generations of mountaineers have asked blessings before attempting Everest.

After the punishment of their race up to the Khumbu Glacier, when he and Mike rejoined the rest of the expedition, Mick Hopkinson felt good to be back with the team and getting on with what they had come to do. For the two of them, though, it was their first day of whitewater after weeks of driving and trekking, and well before the end of the long day, fatigue was catching up. Mick knew he had pushed himself as far as he should for his first day on the river. Leo was filming from high above, though, and holding up the better-acclimatized team was unthinkable as he followed Rob Hastings down a long but unremarkable rapid. Mick reacted too slowly to avoid a recirculating hole, capsized, and as he rolled up his boat broached sideways against a large boulder.

The force of the current instantly piled up, tipping the boat upstream and pinning it against the immobile rock, flattening Mick backward against the rear deck. He could neither release his neoprene sprayskirt nor slide his legs out of the cockpit. The violence of the current hammered him against his boat, the bright, forever unreachable sky just a few green inches above his shoulder. In a desperate surge of adrenaline and anger he tried repeatedly to extricate his body. He was oblivious to the cold, but in fact the glacial water that flowed over his body was chilling it at many times the rate it would have had he been drifting in the same current — the same effect as windchill but vastly quicker. The combination of hypothermia and hypoxia clouded his body and his brain, and, on the very edge of consciousness, he peacefully accepted the inevitable and let go.

In his fog, Mick felt the violence around him increase, his now-limp body whipping in the current like a flag in the wind. And then the building current crushed in the back deck. The broken kayak slid free of the rock, and in one final burst of will and panic, he kicked free of the enclosing fiberglass. Too dazed and weak to swim, he felt himself swept up by waves, battered along the bottom. Mike Jones appeared, chasing him downstream, yelling to pierce his fog, demanding that he swim, that he grab the rope loop on the rear of Mike's kayak. He was able to hold on for a couple of gasping breaths, then they were dragged apart in the tumult. Alternately together and apart, both were swept downstream toward unknown hazards, Mick functioning on instinct alone, on muscle memory learned on the Eiskanal, too stupefied to care, and Mike, still half snow blind, oblivious to the danger as he chased his friend.

Hundreds of feet above on the hillside, Leo Dickinson instinctively focused and framed his big 16mm Arriflex film camera on the struggling figures below, distraught that he was doing nothing to assist, even as he knew there was nothing he could do from that isolated perch. The moment the bright dots of Mike's red kayak and Mick's orange life jacket disappeared from view, he abandoned his camera and pelted downstream, shocked and appalled by the thought that he had probably just filmed Mick's drowning. If that were the case, the film too would be committed to the river.

Mike finally managed to drag Mick, after more than five minutes of immersion and three-quarters of a mile downstream from his pin, into a shoreline eddy, where he floated limp in the water, able only to hang on to a rock to prevent being sucked back into the current. Porters racing downstream from the shore party pulled him onto a beach and began to revive him with dry clothes and hot tea.

The Brits were young, resilient, and perhaps the most aggressive kayakers of their generation. By the next morning dismay had turned into resolve. With his worst fears assuaged, Leo Dickinson wanted not to destroy the film but to add to it, shooting more footage in the same spot to edit into what he rightly expected to be the most dramatic scene of the expedition. Beat-up but game, Mick declared, "You don't spend eighteen months planning a trip like this and give up just because you fall in the water." He scrawled MICK HOPKINSON MARK II across the back deck of a replacement kayak with a felt-tip marker, then joined the others trekking back upstream.

From the outset Mike Jones felt less in control of his kayak than he had the previous day. A compact film camera, about the size of an American football in its clear plastic housing and weighing several pounds, was bolted to his bow. It pushed the bow deeper into holes and waves, where the currents buffeted it with unaccustomed force.

The boat wallowed and stuck in a large hole, the stern sank, the bow bucked straight up, and suddenly he and the boat arced vertically into the air, end over end. When he rolled up he was relieved to find himself clear of the hole but aghast at the unmanageable boat. The modified Bell & Howell Autoload camera and waterproof housing had been custom built in England and completed at the last minute. Testing had not been part of their training sessions on the Eiskanal.

Setting reservations aside, Mike and the other paddlers persevered with the camera system. As far as the adventure-loving British public were concerned, Mike knew, if the team returned without dramatic film they might as well have never been to Everest. In all, they shot slightly more than twenty minutes of "paddler point-of-view" on the Dudh Kosi, obtaining what Leo Dickinson and Mike both considered "the most successful and visually exciting film" of the entire expedition.

The following days brought more risky swims, more broken boats, but nothing as perilous as Mick's pin-and-swim. Evenings in camp they speculated about what sections the Czechs had run, and with what success. The time and resource factors that had plagued them from even before the put-in, however, were now flashing yellow lights. After roughly half of the eighty river miles from the put-in at Pheriche to their objective at the confluence with the Sun Kosi, and 65 percent of the vertical descent, Mike faced a painful dilemma. At the rickety Hillary Bridge, the trail to Kathmandu crossed the Dudh Kosi for the last time and led east to the greater world beyond. Downstream lay their objective, but . . .

Trails continuing down the Dudh Kosi valley had been extensively, and dangerously, cut by landslides the previous winter. There could be neither porter support, rescue climbers, nor film crew below this point. In any case, they had already overspent the porter budget by 300 percent. As on the Inn River seven years previously, boats (that is, fiberglass technology) were again a critical factor. Of the twelve kayaks they had brought from England, nine were either already a write-off or held together only by duct tape. Furthermore, it was now September 23, and most of the team members were scheduled to return to Great Britain, to jobs and families and life obligations, in just a week. From the Sun Kosi confluence, there would be no clear way back to Kathmandu.

As a team they made the painful call, ran one final rapid for the cameras, reorganized the porter loads, and set out on foot for home. For Mike Jones, still smarting from his truncated Blue Nile expedition, this was the second time he had left his dreams, and his promises to supporters, half completed. He was not alone in his disappointment. Leo Dickinson was deeply concerned with the truncated story arc of their film and how that would detract from its drama and commercial success. By the time they reached Kathmandu, Mike and Leo had improvised one final episode to the adventure. Their Everest journey, and their film, had begun with the symbolic trek to set a kayaking altitude record at the nose of the Khumbu Glacier. Leaving the rest of the team to get on with their return to London, Mike and Mick would now fly in to the nearest landing strip and place an exclamation mark at the dramatic confluence where the icy, milk-white Dudh Kosi merged into the mellower golden-brown Sun Kosi River.

Noses pressed to the scratched plastic windows of the Pilatus airplane, Jones, Hopkinson, and Dickinson stared intently into the lower gorges of the Dudh Kosi below. Beneath their wings, the milk-white river raced fifty yards wide between steep, sometimes even undercut, limestone cliffs. With the end of the monsoon season the water levels were now dropping, and the rapids were, as they expected, more spaced out due to the lesser gradient. Thin plumes of smoke indicated small farmsteads and hamlets thousands of feet above the river.

Even with seats unbolted and left behind in Kathmandu, the six-passenger fuselage was crammed to bursting with the three Brits, two kayaks, paddling and camera equipment, a sleeping bag and tarp, and a single rucksack containing several Mars Bars, one packet of raisins, and a few cans of sardines and kippers — the sole remnants of the British Everest Canoe Expedition 1976.

One pass to clear livestock from the incredibly short dirt strip, a white-knuckle landing in a cloud of dust and converging villagers, a wing-wiggle as the Pilatus and Leo vanished over the ridgeline, and Mike and Mick found themselves once more, as in Ethiopia, on their own. The last few miles of the river proved to be flat and fast, and the following afternoon they emerged from the canyon and ferried across the slick Sun Kosi River to a vast sandbar on its right bank. The campsite was idyllic — and there they sat. And sat. Long on ambition and symbolism, Rupert's "plan" was short on detail, such as exactly how they would get home. Leo was to try to charter a helicopter and return for them, but with the end of the rainy season there was pent-up demand for air missions all over the country, and they had no advance reservation. Otherwise, it was going to be a roughly hundred-mile walk out, with only their paddling clothing and bivouac gear. And they had no communications with Leo.

Two days later, against all odds, Leo Dickinson finally chattered in from above, having managed to charter one of just two helicopters then operating from Kathmandu. Before the two paddlers loaded up for their triumphant return, though, Leo insisted they paddle a laborious several hundred yards back up the Dudh Kosi so he could film their "arrival" at the objective from overhead. The scene required three takes, three exhausting slogs up the bankside eddies and against the current. First the helicopter downdraft blew the kayakers out of the water, then the camera angles were wrong. Finally, a wrap.

"That's the best adventure film I have ever seen," blurbed Doug Scott, the first Brit to climb Everest. *Dudh Kosi: Relentless River of Everest* went on to win twenty-five international awards. That was no accident. Dickinson had set out to create a dramatic and therefore successful film, and he did so despite all obstacles and beyond all expectations.

Twenty years earlier on the Indus, Lowell Thomas was the impresario managing his movie production from New York, Otto Lang the director driving each day's activity on their Himalayan "set," Bus and Don Hatch the "stuntmen" enabling the thrilling "scenes." There was no other goal than Cinerama — except perhaps for Peter Parker.

For the Brits on Everest, the film was a genuine partnership — and a marriage of convenience. Mike abetted in every way. He directed expedition activities to conform to the story arc; assumed extra effort and risk with the boat-mounted camera and with repeat takes of critical events; made the rounds on the film and lecture circuit upon return to Great Britain; and perhaps at least condoned an implication that his team were the first down Everest.

"A film is rather like a memory," wrote Dickinson; "you make it reflect the way you would have preferred events to have happened." Rupert's original concept of the expedition, pitched to sponsors, media, and Leo himself, had been to work their way down in or with boats all the way from the nose of the Khumbu Glacier, and thus to have perhaps some claim to a first complete run of the river. That part of the dream died as he and Mick Hopkinson thrashed their way to the outflow of the lake below Everest base camp, then had to walk, snow blind and oxygen-starved, back down the trail to rejoin their team, which had started at the same spot from which the Czechoslovakians had launched three years previously. Yet in his book Leo wrote, "For ten days they had canoed down from the Khumbu Glacier," and the editing and narration of the film imply a continuous run.

Nowhere but in campfire discussions and journal entries was the previous Czech expedition mentioned — not in the film nor in books about the expedition by both Dickinson and Jones. In public, the only evidence that Mike even knew of it is circumstantial but compelling — amid all the hype, he always stopped short of claiming a first descent.

Chris Bonington leans forward, and the timbre of his voice drops with passion as he recalls his friend forty years later. "He was a wonderful role model, really, for true, joyous adventure. He wasn't doing it for fame — he couldn't give a bugger about that . . . and he didn't even get hung up about ethics. (You know, we climbers get all hung up in talking about the climbing ethics.) . . . Mike was taking things to an absolute extreme — but he was doing it for just the sheer joy . . ." The celebrity, the money, were not Rupert's goal, but rather a means to the next high adventure, the next continent, the next demonstration that their nimble kayaks were the perfect tool for river exploration.

For Mike, joy lay not just in the thrill of running big rapids:

> I find it a fascinating experience tackling problems, coming up with solutions and developing the skills and experience to see these through to fruition . . . Each problem requires its own special approach, whether it be puzzling out how to mount a camera on a canoe or persuading a major sponsor to part with a large sum of money . . . Each river has its own special attractions and unique set of problems, whether it be the alligators and piranha fish of a South American river, the thrills and spills of trying to shoot the racing torrents coming off the Himalayas, or the unfriendly natives in the middle of the African jungle.

On the Inn and the Colorado, Mike had been the novice teenager following more experienced leaders. On the Blue Nile and the Dudh Kosi he had followed in the wakes of previous expeditions, learning, sometimes the hard way, to organize and to lead on his own. Now he was determined to jump into the complete unknown.

When Mick Hopkinson flipped through a back issue of the *Geographical* magazine at the boys' middle school where he taught geography, he knew instantly where their next expedition would go. Or at least he knew the answer to that recurring question at the seemingly endless press interviews the paddlers now faced in the wake of the success of Leo Dickinson's film on British national television.

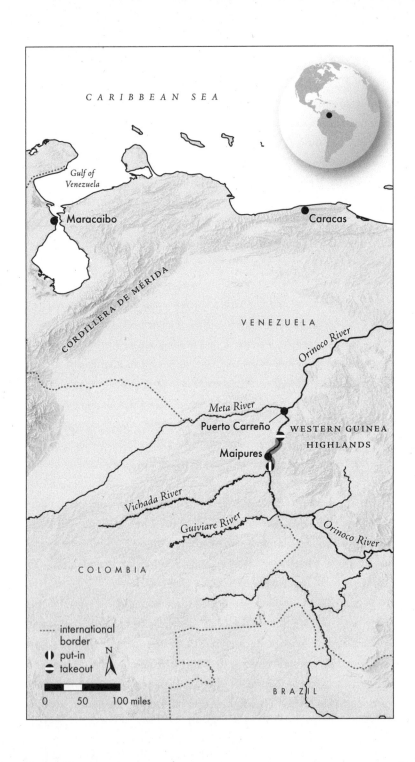

CARIBBEAN SEA

Gulf of
Venezuela

Maracaibo

Caracas

CORDILLERA DE MÉRIDA

VENEZUELA

Orinoco River

Meta River

Puerto Carreño

WESTERN GUINEA

Maipures

HIGHLANDS

Vichada River

Guiviare River

Orinoco River

COLOMBIA

- - - international
      border
❶ put-in
➊ takeout
N

0   50   100 miles

BRAZIL

Spectacular photos showed an eleven-ton, forty-eight-foot hovercraft tossed like a leaf in the wind by gigantic waves in the mile-wide, forty-mile-long Maipure Rapids on the Orinoco River in Venezuela. Just the thing for thirteen-foot kayaks.

Irreverent, sardonic, and ever willing to bait the tabloid press, Mick claimed they would parachute with kayaks into the unexplored jungle headwaters of the Orinoco, then paddle six hundred miles to civilization, their adventure culminating in those "longest in the world" cataracts at Maipure. This was red meat for the ravenous press; there was nothing their latest kayak heroes could not do. Rupert too rose to the bait. Unlike Mick, he took it seriously.

Recruiting companions for such a venture would not be Mike's only challenge. Unlike in the Himalayas, where mountaineering had developed into a lucrative industry, government officials in Venezuela were not accustomed to being asked to embrace unprecedented, high-risk schemes with little purpose but adventure. Access to the remote upper reaches of the Orinoco was restricted to protect the wilderness and the native populations, and Rupert's pleas for special permission went unheeded. The kayakers could come on tourist visas to lower parts of the Orinoco River, including the Maipure Rapids, but they could go no farther.

Despite their success on Everest, or perhaps because of it, major media sponsors did not jump aboard. Leo Dickinson may have made films as he "would have preferred events to have happened," but he understood his niche in the film industry with clear-eyed realism. "The world does not want to be inundated with canoeing films, especially after a particularly good one has been made." CBS in the United States and HTV in Great Britain expressed interest initially and even offered a provisional contract, but by July 1977 talks had stagnated.

Rupert's persistence equaled his audacity. With only tourist visas and shoestring financial support from the *Telegraph Sunday Magazine*, which had also supported Chris Bonington's coverage of the Inn River expedition, British Petroleum, which was invested in South

American oil exploration, and British specialty kayak manufacturer Pyranha, Mike set out for Caracas, Venezuela, in August 1977 to see if he could achieve in person what had proved impossible from afar. With him were Dave Manby and John Gosling from the Everest expedition, Peter Midwood from the Colorado, and newcomer Ronnie Kennedy. As he had done on the Blue Nile and the Dudh Kosi, Mike chose the height of the rainy season, preferring flood to rock, risky swims to broken boats.

For one hundred miles, their rental hatchback bucked and fishtailed through axle-deep red mud, dwarfed by the stack of kayaks and paddles roped onto its roof, its orange paint almost invisible under layers of dust and clay, until they were forced to abandon driving on the inundated roads. Undeterred, the five paddled down the Apure River, a 180-mile tributary of flat water punctuated by getting lost in a maze of meanders and by a surfacing alligator capsizing Peter Midwood. Emerging on the lower Orinoco now miles downstream of their goal, they hired local motorboats to beat their way back upstream, then local trucks to bypass to the head of the Maipure Rapids.

The piranhas were tiny, the alligators middling (by Nile crocodile standards). But the Maipure Rapids were, Mike recalled enthusiastically, "fifty miles long and one mile wide and colossal." Channeled between rocky islands, the flooded river formed huge recirculating holes and trains of exploding haystack waves twenty feet high. Scouting their lines from the distant shores was almost impossible. But there were easier routes as well, places to play and perform for Mike's handheld film camera, to plunge their bows into smaller holes to be tossed vertically end over end, to surf across holes using only their hands. It was an exhilarating two and a half days, and they now had an idea of what the Orinoco had to offer.

Back in Caracas, Mike made the governmental rounds in person, accomplishing in a week what he reckoned would have taken him six months to do by letter from England (if it were possible at all). He talked his way in to see the British ambassador, won him over with his bold plans and boundless enthusiasm — as he had done before with so many others: officials, foundations, commercial sponsors, pilots and baggage handlers, and, of course, fellow kayakers. Through embassy introductions, he was then able to meet and brief the concerned Venezuelan officials, and now he found them interested.

By the time they returned to England, the team had traveled more than ten thousand miles by airplane, auto, motorboat, and kayak. They had spent more than a month away from England, jobs, and family. Of that time, just two and a half days, fifty miles, had been spent whitewater adventuring. This, then, was the reality of genuine first descents, of what separates the true explorers from the vast majority of even highly skilled adventure sportsmen. False starts and reams of paperwork. Endless reconnaissance to discover put-ins and takeouts, to determine ideal water levels and weather conditions. Only then comes the thrill of discovering and overcoming the unknown around every bend. It is axiomatic that whitewater rivers become at least one grade less difficult when the logistics have been worked out and the rapids named — and by then the explorers have moved elsewhere.

Rupert saw the lights turning green, and in October 1977, he filed his formal application to explore the upper Orinoco in 1979. Meanwhile, as the bureaucratic wheels ground slowly in Venezuela, he had the summer of 1978 before him and a world to explore.

From Skardu in northern Pakistan, where Bus Hatch and Otto Lang had finished their first wild ride on the Indus in 1956, Mike and his team trekked north for four days, up the Braldu River gorges, into the Karakoram mountain range. Not yet in sight, but looming over them nevertheless, rose the gigantic ice pyramid of K2, only feet shorter than Everest but more isolated, more dangerous. The ultimate prize, and nightmare, for generations of mountaineers.

As before on the Nile and the Dudh Kosi, Chris Bonington had been able to share with Mike firsthand accounts of the region and the

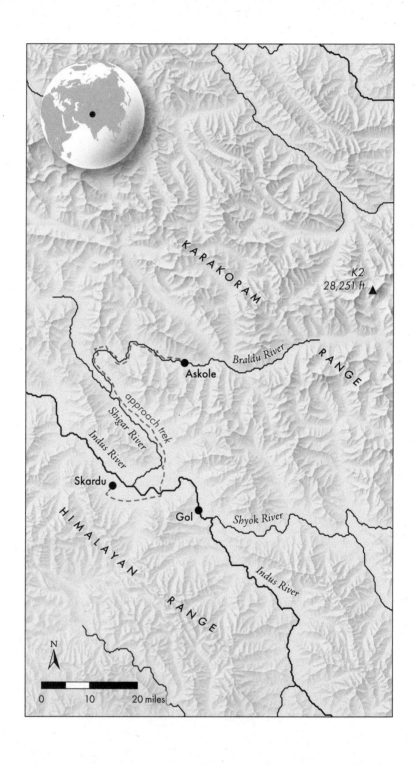

route. Just months before, in May 1978, Bonington had trekked up along the Braldu River to tackle K2. Barely a week into that climb, his best friend, Nick Estcourt, was killed in a massive avalanche, and by consensus the expedition aborted. Bonington nevertheless extolled the savage beauty of the Karakoram, and he detailed for Mike the procedures for obtaining permits, hiring porters, managing the logistics. As with Everest in Nepal, authorities in Pakistan were accustomed to mountaineering expeditions. Rafting and kayaking were not unknown in the region, but they didn't happen often, and never on the Braldu.

Unlike the undulating ridges and tropical valleys of the Everest approach march, their trail climbed steadily along the steep bank of the Braldu River, barren jumbles of glacial rubble and scree, baking shadeless under ninety-degree afternoon temperatures. When lubricated by monsoon deluges, these poorly consolidated hillsides were notorious for landslides, known to pitch travelers to their deaths in the rapids below. The rapids themselves were formed by the fallen rock, not by bedrock ledges, and the paddlers watched in amazement as the flooded riverbed rearranged itself even as they analyzed potential routes.

One day short of their put-in, the team halted at the village of Askole. With good access to the river there, they would take a day to warm up in their boats, to get their sea legs after weeks of punishing travel culminating in the searing trek up from road's end. The warm sun and icy water, direct from the Baltoro Glacier, were sweet relief, dissolving the fatigue and grit of travel as the paddlers got the first taste of their objective. The river was big and powerful, but not extraordinarily difficult; two nasty recirculating holes six to nine feet deep blocked most of the channel but could be skirted both left and right. Through the morning they ran a half-mile section, then carried their kayaks back upstream to repeat — a sweaty process in their neoprene wet suits as the sun rose higher in the cloudless sky. With each run they felt their familiar skills returning, the intimidation of the churning gray Braldu abating.

Mike was eager to get some paddling footage on film for the BBC and to test for the first time a new helmet-mounted camera to get those point-of-view shots that had proved so successful in *Dudh Kosi: Relentless River of Everest*. After a lunch break, he returned to the river with Roger Huyton and Dave Manby to "put some in the can." With the air temperature now in the nineties, Mike abandoned his sweaty wet suit, to which he had a lifetime aversion because it constricted his movement, even while he admitted its protective value. Buckling on a motorcycle helmet mounted with an eleven-pound camera-and-battery combination, he followed the other two downstream, filming as they approached the massive midstream stoppers.

The river beneath their hulls had changed. The sweltering midday sun was also melting the giant glacier upstream, and with unexpected power the swollen current seized the two kayaks ahead and flung them to the center of the river. Realizing the danger, Dave Manby powered desperately to his left and barely skirted the hole; Roger Huyton aimed right and failed. Thrashed for nearly a minute in the hole, he finally exited his boat and washed downstream into the unknown beyond where they had practiced that morning. As he had for Mick Hopkinson on the Dudh Kosi, Mike raced downstream in pursuit, heedless to the risks of paddling such water blindly, of the eleven-pound weight on his head that would make an Eskimo roll virtually impossible, and of his lack of protection from the glacial cold if he swam.

Mike caught up to the swimmer, who was briefly able to seize the rescue loop on the stern of his kayak. Before Mike could tow him ashore, however, they were swept into yet another massive hole and pulled apart. "That was the last I saw of Mike. When I surfaced again his boat was bobbing crazily away, upside down." Roger Huyton washed into a shoreline eddy. There was never a trace of Mike, only the full force of the Braldu pounding into sheer rock on river left downstream, dangerously undercut.

Rupert's teammates abandoned the Karakoram and raced back to England to share their grief with Mike's family. To this day his sister

Chris takes comfort from Mick Hopkinson's account of his own near fatality on the Dudh Kosi and his description of whitewater hypothermia as a peaceful letting go.

On July 30, 1980, in private audience at Buckingham Palace, Queen Elizabeth II presented Mike's parents, Reg and Molly Jones, his posthumous Queen's Gallantry Medal in recognition of that doomed rescue attempt.

Parachuting into the Orinoco jungles was not to be.

CHAPTER SIX

Catholicism and Communism in Earth's Grandest Cathedral

The Colca River

It is always hard to see the purpose in wilderness
wanderings until after they are over.
— John Bunyan, *The Pilgrim's Progress*

The blue-and-white Chevy pickup rolled across the Peruvian alti-plano, dust billowing in the thin air above thirteen thousand feet, the fine grit caking passengers, boats, and gear alike. On the far horizons, the snow-covered volcanic peaks of the Central Andean Cordillera, Nevado Mismi being the highest at 18,363 feet, glistened. Behind the travelers stretched two years and thousands of miles traversing three continents. Ahead lay one of the deepest, most inaccessible, and least-known river canyons on the planet. At Chivay, the last major town they would encounter before throwing themselves into the Colca Canyon, six young Polish adventurers found lodging with the nuns of the local church and made final preparations for the culmination of a quixotic expedition.

Over the sisters' battery-operated shortwave radio, on May 13, 1981, they heard devastating news. Crackling across the airwaves from a Warsaw radio studio seven thousand miles away, an announcer's voice intoned in Polish: "Ladies and gentlemen, I am holding in my hand a message, which I would never want to hold in my life." Earlier that day, a crazed Turkish gunman had attempted to assassinate Pope John Paul II in Rome. Wounded three times, the pope lay fighting for his life in a hospital, and from early reports he was not expected to live. This was their own *Papiez z Polski* (pope from Poland), native son of their hometown, Kraków, their own Cardinal Karol Wojtyla! Not only did he embody the deep and abiding Catholic faith of Poland, which coexisted undaunted alongside the communist state, but he was a skier, a mountaineer, and yes, a kayaker. To these young men he demonstrated that outdoor adventure and religious faith could be mutually supporting, that glory was to be found in the mountains as well as in cathedrals. Their reverence for their hero *Papiez* surpassed mere admiration.

Heartsick, the Poles climbed into their bedrolls, communing silently with their innermost thoughts — and fears. Jerzy Majcherczyk fell into a deep sleep and dreamed: He lay prostrate, arms extended to form a cross — a penitent's pose. Cold engulfed his body from an icy concrete floor, and, behind his head, he somehow knew, ornate church walls rose to disappear into roiling clouds. He woke shivering in the thin mountain air, unable to shake his ominous vision.

Homesick for family and country after more than two years on the road, kayaker Andrzej Piętowski lay awake and reflected on the trials and near misses his team had already experienced in running nineteen rivers, many of them first descents, in North, Central, and South America. Their equipment was worn out, their funds depleted, their food supply scant. And inescapably, the completely unknown loomed ahead, a run more daunting than anything they had yet encountered: sandwiched between near-vertical walls soaring ten thousand feet above their heads, on a river cascading four thousand feet down a boulder-choked streambed that there was no record of anyone having even attempted to run.

In the next few days, would they realize the ultimate triumph they had first dared to dream four years before, or would they fatally overreach, the price for their hubris? The tragedy unfolding for their faith and their homeland as their hero pope struggled to survive seemed foreboding given the unknowable risks they were about to

plunge into and made their grand ambitions suddenly seem trivial
. . . to what end?

Well over two years before, on the other side of the Atlantic, Kraków, Poland, like its Warsaw Pact neighbor Ostrava, Czechoslovakia, had endured under an industrial pall of coal and diesel soot and communist bureaucracy. And like Jiří Bobák and his team five years earlier, these restless students at Kraków's University of Mining and Metallurgy had sought escape in the freedom and individualism of whitewater sports. Somehow they too obtained loan of a military truck to go whitewater adventuring. But there the similarities ended, and the dream concocted in 1977 by Jerzy "Yurek" Majcherczyk, Andrzej Piętowski, and Piotr Chmieliński was to work out quite differently from the meticulously planned, led, and executed Czechoslavakian expedition to Mount Everest.

These Polish undergraduates were hardly the elite of the whitewater world. A few years before, Yurek Majcherczyk had cofounded the Bystrze [Rapids] Canoe Club. It quickly grew to four hundred members, chiefly by offering trips running rivers in Yugoslavia and other nearby countries behind the Iron Curtain — a refreshing alternative to the highly regimented and politically oriented activities available to students through Communist Party organizers. Nor were they zealous representatives to the rest of the world of communist Poland or Polish paddle sports tradition. While Poland did have some good individual paddlers, its racing teams did not dominate medal platforms as did the Germans, the Czechoslovakians, and the Yugoslavs. The Poles had nothing to prove.

With graduation looming followed by entry into a dour adult world of duty — of military service, of family obligations with marriages and children, of devout Catholic faith, and of solid but predictable professional careers within the State — Chmieliński proposed one last, ultimate, road trip. He had been reading about South America, its soaring Andes Mountains and its dark remote jungles. It did not matter to them that they were students with neither money nor experience outside Eastern Europe, or that both the Iron Curtain and the Atlantic Ocean lay between them and their road trip destination, or that much of the region was consumed by political unrest and conflict. All the adventure and romance they yearned for awaited them in unexplored regions of South America. With unlimited faith and determination, they resolved to take their kayaks to Argentina.

The first, almost imperceptible swells of change that would soon crest in the Warsaw Pact countries as Glasnost and Perestroika and, specific to Poland, Solidarity, must have already begun pulsing through the Polish bureaucracy, for after two years of preparation and applications, the students were granted permission to travel. Throughout the Soviet bloc, sports were propaganda, and one of the non-negotiable conditions of their travel visas was that their expedition would be documented with still and video photography. After overcoming the bureaucratic hurdles of communist Eastern Europe, however, they then had to contend with the volatile geopolitics of Latin America. As they prepared their ten-member team — six kayakers, cinematographer, photographer, shuttle driver, and physician — their twenty-one kayaks, and their loaner military truck for the sea voyage from Poland to Argentina, tensions flared in a long-standing border dispute between Argentina and Chile, and their visas were abruptly canceled.

Thwarted but undaunted, they turned their sights to Peru. Chmieliński had read an article about the remote and almost impossibly deep Colca Canyon. It had only been revealed to modern geographers by aircraft observation; no record existed of penetration since the Inca era. The Rio Colca cut its dramatic gorge an astonishing two and a half vertical miles below the 17,146-foot peak of Sena Yajirhua on river right, two vertical miles below the 13,967-foot peak of Cerro Luceria on the left. It was thought at the time to be the deepest canyon on the planet. They hastily obtained visas for Peru and prepared to launch. But then, in the deep winter of 1979–80, the North Sea froze solid, and as they waited for shipping to resume, their luck ran out again. Amid increasing violence surrounding a bitter contest to oust Peru's ruling military junta at the ballot box, and the emergence of the Shining Path communist insurgency, their visas were revoked. For the Bystrze Canoe Club's Canoandes Expedition, it was now any port in a storm. In desperation, they managed to obtain Mexican visas, and, after two years of preparation and a ten-month delay in departure, they dispatched all their gear on a Polish freighter bound for the Mexican Atlantic port of Tampico.

Somehow, in that restless night on the altiplano, Chmieliński's doubts abated; he woke to a brilliant chill dawn and with a renewed sense of resolve. For their gravely wounded hero pope and for their grieving nation, all they could do was pray. But they were poised on the cusp of a great adventure, the verge of either discovery or tragedy. The red-and-white Polish flag and the photo of John Paul II that had adorned their truck across North, Central, and South America now represented something more than an ambitious end-of-term adventure for a group of university friends. An assassin in Rome had transformed it into a test of their courage and pride as Poles, and a symbol for the indomitable spirit of the pope himself.

As they gathered around the cookstove, numbed hands wrapped around steaming mugs of coffee, Chmieliński could sense, without a word being said, that his companions all shared his renewed determination. Each, in his own way, felt the pull of history. Their time had come to move forward, into the abyss.

On the morning of May 18, 1981, an eerie silence filled the canyon as the six who now constituted the Canoandes Expedition watched the last burro and driver disappear back up the ancient Inca foot trail to the canyon rim sixty-five hundred feet above their heads. They were now totally alone with the plunging river and the soaring broken rock. There would be no human presence for twenty-four miles, just

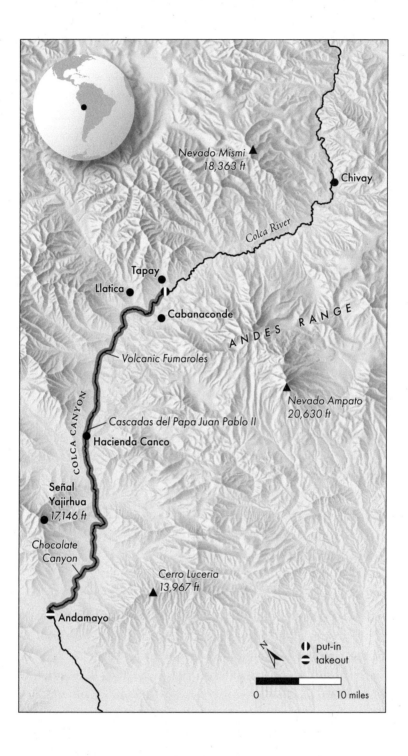

Nevado Mismi
18,363 ft

Chivay

Colca River

Tapay

Llatica

Cabanaconde

ANDES RANGE

Volcanic Fumaroles

Nevado Ampato
20,630 ft

Cascadas del Papa Juan Pablo II

Hacienda Canco

COLCA CANYON

Señal
Yajirhua
17,146 ft

Chocolate
Canyon

Cerro Luceria
13,967 ft

Andamayo

( ) put-in
( ) takeout

N

0   10 miles

condors gliding silently high above, and thorny vegetation dotting a barren landscape. The simplicity of their task ahead was both a relief from the myriad difficulties in getting to this start point and a chilling reminder of their exposure. An injury, or the loss of critical equipment like the raft, could endanger them all. Their only, tenuous, link to the outside world was Javier Ford, the team's newest recruit, from Lima, who would remain with the truck above and respond as needed. Without radio or other electronic link, however, they would be entirely dependent upon human messengers to communicate.

Eager to finally get on the water, Andrzej Piętowski and Piotr Chmieliński shouldered their torn, patched, broken-and-repaired-again fiberglass kayaks and clambered down the last several hundred feet of steep bank to the river, then returned to help manhandle the raft, boxes of food, and other supplies — foreshadowing hundreds of such carries they were to face downstream.

Jacek Bogucki shot film, scrambling between vantage points on the sunbaked rocky hillsides. Filming and photographing their exploits was such an important goal that they had scrimped on food and repairs for the truck to buy film. Short on cash, they had bartered climbing ropes to hire the burros that transported their gear into the canyon. And Jacek was now on his own. Photographer Zbigniew Bzdak, with the team from the beginning, shooting each of the nineteen rivers they had run so far, lay frustrated and bedridden with malaria in Lima as his companions approached their culminating adventure.

As the others lashed their bulky gear into the raft, securing heavy items in a net above the rubber floor to prevent tearing as it slid over rocks, Yurek Majcherczyk stretched a climbing rope across the river to measure its width. With a pole, he sounded the depth, and by timing a floating stick over a measured distance he determined the velocity of the flow. By assuming a V-shaped river bottom, he made a field-expedient calculation of the Rio Colca's flow: 650 to 700 cubic feet per second. That flow was not really adequate to ensure clearance in the steep, technical riverbed, especially for the raft, but they had no choice. They knew of no other access until halfway through the canyon, and the dry season was upon them. Delay would just make matters worse. The water temperature measured fifty degrees Fahrenheit, and from their rough Peruvian map, he estimated the altitude to be seventy-two hundred feet. Together with the photography, these measurements, to be repeated at stages during their descent, and detailed journals, often recorded nightly by candlelight as exhausted companions slept, had been their ticket around the world. A guidebook the Bystrze Canoe Club had compiled of rivers in Yugoslavia had impressed Polish authorities with their seriousness and potential value to the state. In Mexico data and reports presented to that country's minister of tourism resulted in both financial support and, more important, letters of introduction throughout Central and South America. Those letters, combined with a coat and necktie carefully folded in the bottom of each man's kit for meetings with officials, opened doors as they traveled south. They took themselves seriously and were taken seriously in return.

The sole exception to the success of their public image campaign came in Honduras, whose government was locked in a brutal counter-insurgency against communist guerrillas. They were only grudgingly allowed forty-eight hours to transit the country nonstop. In the end they wound up traversing twenty-two countries, running rivers in all but Honduras.

Two unlikely recent recruits to the expedition, Stefan Danielski and Krzysztof "Biczu" Kraśniewski, rounded out the team of six now alone at the bottom of the canyon. Fellow Poles and equally adventur-ous, they were not rivermen at all but merchant mariners, off on their own grand adventure before settling into the strictures of adulthood, working their way around the globe. They had fallen in with the Cano-andes team on a Polish freighter that transported the explorers around the Darién Gap, the roadless missing link in the Pan-American High-way between Panama and Colombia, and the two put their round-the-world romp on hold in Ecuador to chase the river dreams of their new companions. They had no previous experience whitewater rafting, and now their fate would lie primarily in the hands of Yurek Majcherczyk, who would captain the raft they rode.

Andrzej Piętowski drifted ahead of the raft, leapfrogging with Piotr Chmieliński to scout the rapids and signal the way downstream for Yurek. The afternoon was everything Andrzej had dreamed of. In his kayak he felt safe, able to stop in an instant, his fate in his own paddle — not in the condition of road and truck, nor the whim of government officials, nor the recalcitrant burros who had brought them down into the canyon. Barren walls of multihued granites and volcanics rose a dizzying two miles on either side. Drop followed exhilarating drop every few hundred feet. They took their time, savoring the wonder of the surroundings, filming and photographing. A sharp late-day wind swept up the canyon, slowing the raft, and by four in the afternoon the sun had long since disappeared behind the canyon walls as they made camp on a rocky bench on river right. In just two hours on the water, they had made three miles of progress downstream. A hearty dinner of canned vegetable soup, canned meat and rice, topped off with a shot of rum, culminated an idyllic day.

These were not the same paddlers who had first come to the New World twenty-three months and nineteen rivers ago, who had called themselves Canoandes '79 even though in 1979 they were still stuck in Poland, and, when they finally did begin their expedition, had been on an entirely different continent from the Andes Mountains. Early on, when they were newly arrived in Mexico, the Pescados River had been a rude warm-up. At the end of a long day of countless swims, seven of their twenty-one kayaks were either smashed or lost altogether. Faith and optimism could no longer obscure the facts that only three of the paddlers were experienced beyond "intermediate" levels of whitewater, and none had reliable Eskimo rolls.

The lesson Piotr Chmieliński took away from the Pescados River was that, as their mission at the moment was to run rivers, they must become tougher, bolder, and better paddlers. In his uninhibited vision, the best place to carry that out, fortunately within driving range even at their top speed of thirty-five miles per hour, was the Grand Canyon of the Colorado in the United States. A former member of the Bystrze Canoe Club in Kraków had emigrated to Casper, Wyoming. They would head there and regroup.

The young Poles were hardworking, fun loving, good company. A delighted *Casper Star-Tribune* greeted them and their lumbering, six-wheeled military truck (top speed thirty-five miles per hour) with the headline: INVASION OF WARSAW PACT. They were warmly welcomed and settled in for a winter of odd jobs to replenish their meager funds. The charm that had inveigled travel permits and an army truck from the communist government of Poland, and entry visas from the United States authorities, failed with the US National Park Service, however. Grand Canyon runs were closed off for the winter, and the rangers, who perhaps saw at a glance how ill equipped they were, were disinclined to grant an exception. No permit was forthcoming. They settled for runs of Marble Canyon and the Wind River, then headed back to Mexico — via Las Vegas, San Francisco, and Los Angeles, since they were in the neighborhood.

Their winter sojourn resulted in little river experience, but it had proved a boon to their finances and logistics. Their laborers' wages in US dollars were many times those of a skilled engineer or other professional back in Poland, and with the expedition coffers replenished they were able to purchase a professional-quality fourteen-foot Riken whitewater raft in San Francisco to carry gear on multiday runs and so the non-paddling photographers could accompany the river team. It was the most up-to-date of all their equipment. No one on the expedition had ever paddled a raft of any sort.

And in Las Vegas they hit a true jackpot, in the form of a chance encounter with a family of expatriate Polish acrobats. The Jabczynski Troupe were described by a contemporary circus performer as "strong as bulls. They worked hard and played hard. That Polish vodka from the embassy had a kick." They were so taken with their amiable young countrymen's sense of adventure that they not only took them in and showed them the town (as only insiders can know it) but also remained loyal fans and supporters, providing moral and material support for the duration of the adventure.

Back in Mexico, the team resumed their quest, working their way down, and documenting, several more Mexican rivers. On the Santa Maria, where the iconic Tamul Falls drops nearly three hundred feet directly into the Santa Maria gorge in a riot of spume and rainbow-tinted mist, steep boulder-choked labyrinths tested their limits at every bend and foreshadowed what awaited in the Colca Canyon, three thousand miles south and months in their future. Like the Pescados, their run on the Santa Maria had not gone well for them. Only nine of the fourteen days were devoted to paddling, the rest to untangling themselves from difficulties: Twenty-one portages impressed upon them the downside to their newly acquired raft, and a flip of the raft resulted in the loss of all their food. They had to subsist the last four days on a single catfish they were able to trap in the shallows.

Each struggling step forward in Mexico was followed by a seemingly terminal setback and then by miraculous intervention. The Polish government had had enough. They were instructed to return the lumbering Warsaw Pact military truck via the Mexican port of Vera-cruz. Their dreams of South America seemed dashed. But rather than let this end their odyssey, it became the catalyst to refine their group of student adventurers into a leaner, more effective expedition. Learning of the expedition's imminent termination by Polish authorities, their new but loyal friends, the expatriate Jabczynski Troupe of acrobats in Las Vegas, unexpectedly donated a quintessential American Chevrolet Cheyenne pickup truck. As half the team returned to Poland with the original truck, the three most experienced paddlers, Yurek Majcher-czyk, Andrzej Piętowski, and Piotr Chmieliński, together with cine-matographer Jacek Bogucki and photographer Zbyszek Bzdak, would continue in their Chevy, now sporting a salvage yard camper back, a

platform trailer, a large red-and-white Polish flag, and a portrait of
Pope John Paul II provided by Yurek's mother to watch over them in
their travels. They were back on plan.

As they proceeded down the spine of the Americas, with each run,
each hard lesson, their whitewater skills developed, even as their dwindling number of fiberglass kayaks and their formerly new raft deteriorated. They had left Poland as exceptionally bold and athletic young
men; now with each new country, each new river, they became tough
as well, resistant to cold and heat, to bad food, to altitude. And they
developed a solidarity that had not been possible with the larger, more
diverse group. Shared hardship and danger had deepened a communal
sense of purpose and determination — which would soon be tested.

On the second day, the Colca closed like a vise.

Immediately below camp the river dropped fifteen or twenty feet
in a slalom of narrow drops over the next five hundred feet. Jacek and
Stefan scrambled down the right bank to an overlook from which they
could film the whole sequence. Andrzej and Piotr took their places
in the raft for a smooth run down, then hiked back upstream to their
kayaks. Almost from the start Piotr lost his line, capsized, missed two
Eskimo rolls, and swam. Krzysztof threw him a rescue rope; Andrzej,
in his kayak, chased down Piotr's paddle; Yurek and Stefan jumped
into the river and wrestled the swamped kayak to the left bank; and
Jacek filmed all the drama. Within seconds all was again safe and under
control — but as Yurek and Stefan went to empty Piotr's swamped
boat, water gushed from a gaping split along the vulnerable seam joining the fiberglass hull to the deck. That kayak was going no farther
without major repair.

The group halted and set the damaged kayak in the sun to bake
dry, as Piotr readied the only repair kit they had: a roll of American
duct tape. If applied carefully to a perfectly dry surface, on a bias to
the split seam, this would provide at least a temporary watertight seal.

The slightest moisture from the torn fiberglass, however, would ruin the adhesion, and it would fall off in minutes. The process could not be rushed. This was the first time they had been immersed for any length of time in the Colca's glacier-fed water. The paddlers welcomed the opportunity to strip off their soaked cotton clothing and stretch out naked to bask like lizards on the hot rocks. The searing sun was edging toward the canyon rim, however, and they needed to keep moving. Piotr completed his duct-tape repair, and they reembarked, Yurek impatiently leading the way in the raft. The river steepened, the rapids became more closely spaced, choked with sharp, angular rock newly fallen from walls that overhung the narrow waterway from both sides, almost touching a hundred feet above their heads. No sunlight penetrated; they continued in a stygian gloom.

The river necked down to a channel about twenty feet wide, then split around a massive blade of rock. On the right, a ten-foot vertical drop fell directly into a cauldron barely bigger than the raft, the exit downstream blocked by a sieve of sharp rocks — no room for raft or human. In contrast, the narrow slot on the left would be an easy slide. It was a must-catch move — and they did not make it happen. Just before the boulder that split the channel, the front of the raft hung up on an unseen, shallow rock; the raft swung to the right and dropped sideways into the trap below, spilling Yurek, Jacek, Biczu, and Stefan helter-skelter.

Fear would come later. Shocked by the icy water, Yurek came to his senses in a concussed welter of dark tumbling water and consuming guilt. The raft, their only means to continue down the river; the climbing ropes that might permit escape; and their entire supply of food and camp gear were capsized, perhaps lost. Yurek was captain of the raft. How could he have missed seeing that shallow rock, allowed the unthinkable to happen? Put all his companions into this deadly trap?

Yurek's immediate situation, however, was dire. The capsized raft blocked him from the surface, from the air and light. Currents like giant hands clawed at his body, tugging downward. He clung to a mooring rope as the raft bucked in the cauldron. On the verge of drowning, he pulled himself to the front of the raft and miraculously found an air pocket. His breath and wits somewhat recovered, he dove and emerged beside the raft. Beside him, Biczu too tumbled in the hole, shouting for help each time he surfaced in the recirculation. Then, perhaps because of some subtle change in the hydrodynamics, the raft broke free of its entrapment, washing downstream and pulling Yurek and Biczu in its wake. Still clinging to the mooring rope, Yurek struggled desperately for a purchase with his feet, but the swamped raft pulled him inexorably downstream, slamming him into underwater rocks. From the front, Jacek vainly tried to block the momentum as well. Andrzej splashed out to join, and together they finally managed to wrestle the raft and sodden cargo ashore.

Andrzej and Biczu pelted back upstream in search of Stefan, still trapped under the initial drop, clinging to a rock ledge to avoid being sucked back into the recirculation, too exhausted to aid himself. On the second cast, Stefan caught Andrzej's rescue rope, tied it fast around his waist, and pendulumed to the shore. He emerged to safety naked but for his torn T-shirt, his pants and life jacket torn off during the churning. Dazed and battered, they had no choice but to regroup and proceed downstream through the sunless tunnel.

The river turned, and the walls widened in a blaze of sunlight. Above their heads appeared a suspension bridge, steep footpaths switchbacking up either wall, linking villages invisible to them far above. Jacek climbed to the bridge to film the others running an easy rapid below, then rejoined the raft as they continued downstream to a camp at the green confluence of the tributary Rio Llatica.

A realization of the price they could have paid sank in almost the moment they stopped paddling. Stefan and Jacek were exhausted and numbed by their swims. Jurek shook with exhaustion. His hip and elbow were painfully bruised, both hands rope-burned. In the aftermath of his concussion, his balance was shaky, and he suffered brief hallucinations as he made his camp on a flat rock by the water's edge. But there was satisfaction too, and an extra sense of camaraderie around the cookstove. They had been tested, and their team had emerged unbowed.

The next day equipment repairs, this time the pump to inflate the raft, again consumed the morning, and once they launched, the rock-choked riverbed served up more brutally hard labor. Fewer rapids were runnable. Time-consuming scouting from shore was now the norm, followed frequently by difficult lining of the empty raft down the sieve-like rapids with climbing ropes, fighting to maintain their footing on the wet rock against the pull of the river, knowing that a dropped rope could spell disaster.* Occasionally the entire river disappeared under rockfalls, and four men had to shoulder the 175-pound raft to stumble over the rubble. Their rigid box of food and cooking equipment was almost as awkward. Progress downstream was measured in just yards per hour, not miles. When they made camp, Yurek calculated that they had advanced less than two miles that day, and less than six from the put-in.

On the morning of the fourth day came Andrzej's turn on the other end of the throw-rope. Half a mile of navigable rapids ended at a longer, steeper drop — right on the borderline of their abilities even to attempt. Mindful of his split-and-duct-taped seam, Piotr decided immediately to carry and set off down the shoreline. Andrzej thought he saw a line and elected to run. The raft crew watched from above to see how it went. In the middle of the rapid, Andrzej overturned, and as the hull of the kayak swept downstream the rafters could see nothing of Andrzej, neither attempting to roll up nor swimming. Without hesitation they pushed out into the current and made chase. They nearly came to grief as well, filling the raft with water in a hole, then

---

* Lining is a technique to lower an empty raft or canoe down a rapid, controlling it from shore by utilizing long ropes attached to bow and stern. Adjusting the relative lengths of the lines sets the angle of the boat and allows it to be driven laterally across the current. Lining is seldom used with kayaks, given their much greater ease of portage.

pinning against a midstream rock. They managed to extricate themselves and make shore just as Andrzej's swamped kayak floated by.

Yurek tied a throw-rope around his waist and dove in after it, but
in vain. The shards of torn fiberglass he recovered would run no more
rapids, and Andrzej was now the fifth passenger in the raft.

Opening the food chest to prepare dinner that evening, Yurek was
dismayed to discover it full of water from the pin that morning. Sugar,
rice, pasta, oatmeal, and matches all were soaked. Taking stock, they
realized that with the kayak they had also lost their backup supply of
matches, and, of less immediate concern, the entire remaining expedition money supply — roughly two hundred US dollars. Among
them they had a total of one dollar and sixty-nine cents. Dinner was
cold soup, tea, and their last can of meat, sliced into six exactly equal
cutlets, and in the morning their start was again delayed, this time to
dry the sodden food and matches when the sun finally penetrated to
the floor of the canyon.

When they finally launched, the river was even more constricted
than before, and backbreaking, ankle-twisting portages followed
one after another. In camp, at the end of that long fifth day, veterans Andrzej, Piotr, Jerzy, and Jacek spoke openly the thought that had
been haunting each. They were in trouble. They had already lost one
kayak, and twice they had nearly lost the indispensable raft and food
supplies.

Just as dire as their precarious boat situation was their dwindling
ration supply. They had launched with a seven-, perhaps eight-day
quantity of canned goods and whatever staples they could buy in local
markets — a quantity dictated by the need to not overload the small
raft and based on their experience of running sixty-mile distances on
other rivers during their odyssey. Even so, the food and camp equipment weighed more than three hundred pounds when they started.*

---

* Lightweight, compact freeze-dried rations were first developed for US special operations forces in Vietnam in the mid-1960s. Not unlike the World War II surplus rubber
rafts that had revolutionized whitewater rafting in the 1950s, the Long Range Patrol

Now most of the food was consumed. They had already run out of fuel for the cookstove, and combustible vegetation was scarce.

They had penetrated just ten miles into the Colca Canyon, an average of two miles per day. Before them lay roughly another fifty miles. Hacienda Canco, the only known habitation within the gorge where they might find food, still lay fifteen miles downstream. A more revealing measure of their progress, the vertical, was even more concerning. They had — at great cost to their bodies, their equipment, and their supplies — run, lined, and portaged down roughly twelve hundred vertical feet so far. The mouth of the canyon lay yet another three thousand and more feet below. The thrill of whitewater adventure was over, and, Yurek admitted to himself, the struggle to stay alive had begun. He looked up to the narrow slit of sky above and prayed to God for help, for something to get them out of rock hell before they ran out of food and energy.

What, then, could get them from this sandy ledge to the mouth of the Colca Canyon? Disciplined and linear in his approach to any situation, Piotr tuned out his doubts and focused on the steps. Not what could they do, but what must they do. First, they must reach Hacienda Canco, where they likely would find food. From there, they could resupply, repair, heal, and prepare for the second section of the canyon: longer, deeper, with greater flow of water.

And to reach Hacienda Canco they must speed up. However, they could not do so by taking more risk, by neglecting scouting or running more dangerous rapids. They had paid the price already for faulty judgments — and they were lucky they had lost only one kayak and no lives. From here on their decisions, individual and collective, must be infallible.

(LRP) rations were marketed to mountaineering and other expeditions under the Mountain House brand beginning in 1969. No such thing was available behind the Iron Curtain when the Canoandes team launched, nor in the hinterlands of Peru as they provisioned for the Colca Canyon. Even had they been available, they would have been beyond the meager Canoandes budget.

At the same time, Andrzej knew that this was the challenge they had dreamed of so many miles ago in Kraków. As university students, he and his friends had no goal to mount the medal platforms in world racing competition, nor to run the most difficult rapids ever run, nor to drop the highest waterfall. They had no thought to leverage movie or television coverage for high-tech equipment, helicopter scouting, and media fame. Rather, they were pursuing the romance of exploration itself: to throw themselves into the unknown, to test their faith and fortitude with whatever skills and assets they had available, and to emerge to reveal new knowledge to the world. Specifically, Canoandes sought to explore never-before-run rivers and canyons and to publish guidebooks and films for other sportsmen to follow. Now, for better or worse, they had found all that.

One thing all six knew: Only teamwork could speed them up, keep them safe, get them out. They knew the countless stories of mountaineering and polar expeditions that had fragmented and failed, often with fatal results. The harder things got, the more they must support one another, avoid quarrels, pull together. The Canoandes was an expedition without a formal leadership structure. Andrzej was named their leader in public, in large part because he had the best skills in English and Spanish and so could best represent them in government, media, and other social interactions. Yurek commanded the raft, with its five men and all-important cargo. Piotr led by his example, his cool judgment, and his self-discipline. Jacek managed the filming, and newcomers Stefan and Biczu were mostly silent partners, willing to try anything, endure anything. This ad-hoc leadership had served them well — so far. Now it must get them at least seventeen more miles to Hacienda Canco, and ideally the full fifty-four to the mouth of the Colca Canyon.

They fought their way downstream on half rations, and just as the rock walls had closed on them like a vise, so too did hunger, cold, and illness. They wore only thin cotton shirts and trousers, had not anticipated the glacial melt nor the rapid chill of the high-altitude desert when the sun disappeared. By day they talked of food, their favorite dishes, what would be their first meals back in Lima. By night they shivered in thin sleeping bags on narrow rock ledges, dreaming restlessly of avalanching cliffs and of drifting helplessly toward roaring waterfalls. The days blended in a fog of exhaustion, hunger, cold, pain, and sensory overload.

They passed under another hanging bridge — the last they would see, they learned from three crossing Indians, before Hacienda Canco. Jacek filmed from the bridge as the others passed below, then scrambled down to rejoin the paddlers. There was no discussion of abandoning the river and walking out.

Yurek had been tormented for days by dry and itching skin, and now feverish chills alternated with hot sweats. He noted wryly in his daily journal that the hot sweats were his only relief from the interminable itch.

They camped at a rare, sandy beach with plentiful driftwood deposited by the previous rainy season floods. Flickers of light from their bonfire illuminated soaring canyon walls like an enormous cathedral, its dark indigo ceiling punctuated with hundreds of crystalline stars.

They rounded a corner and were assailed with the rotten-egg smell of sulfur. Fumaroles, limed with deposits in shades of reds, greens, and browns, hissed steam from the rock walls, and by the banks the river boiled. Hot springs called to their aching bodies like sirens, but hunger demanded that they pass on.

The river disappeared entirely beneath a gigantic rockslide. Boulders the size of buildings blocked the full width of the canyon for at least five hundred yards. Teaming up to carry the raft and kitchen box was impossible; they hauled both up each gargantuan block of broken stone with climbing ropes, then lowered them down the other side, repeating this laborious process for five hours throughout the afternoon.

They ate their last rice, their last can of fish. Only a few packaged biscuits and crackers, tea, and damp sugar remained.

A slip on wet rock while lining the raft down yet another steep drop, a line jerked from Yurek's hands, and the raft plunged out of control, to be crushed under tons of water cascading over a vertical falls. Still attached on the downstream line, Stefan and Andrzej, joined by the others, finally wrestled the swamped raft to shore, only to discover half of its floor ripped loose from the body. No repair was possible with their rudimentary supplies, yet they had no choice but to proceed downstream, the raft now awkward to sit in and to steer.

Dinner was one damp biscuit each, washed down with sugared tea. That was the last of the solid food.

Andrzej nursed a painful toothache, then his left eye became inflamed. With his semi-blindness came a vertigo that made scrambling up and down the rocks difficult. On rock-strewn beaches, they sought out separate niches for their bedrolls, where each could nurse his wounds without revealing his weakness to the others.

Before them the next morning, the whole river pitched down dramatically. Over five hundred yards, the Colca cascaded down roughly two hundred feet in a series of falls, the highest a vertical drop of more than sixty feet. A rumble like passing railroad cars, and the screeching of their brakes, reverberated off cliffs that bounded the flow on its left — an infinity of horizontal striations shot through with the grays and icy blues of a glacial crevasse. Aquamarine water dissolved into plunging curtains of dazzling white. Plumes of mist, shot with rainbows where the sun penetrated the canyon, sparkled like stained glass. And beyond, painting the hillside in brilliant sunlight high above the far shore, the sight they had not seen for eleven days: the verdant green of vegetation, of cultivation, of Hacienda Canco, of life.

More important even than the corn, cheese, and two protein-rich eggs apiece that the villagers were able to provide the emaciated Poles that night was a crumpled, days-old newspaper from beyond the canyon rim. The pope had survived! Their beloved countryman and patron saint was expected to fully recover. All their prayers answered, they spontaneously decided to name the falls that had led them here that afternoon, the most spectacular place they had experienced so far, the Cascadas del Papa Juan Pablo II. All six were wounded and debilitated by disease and malnutrition. Both the raft and the one surviving kayak required repairs with material obtainable only in major cities. Even their remaining footgear and clothing were worn to the point of falling off. And the tiny subsistence village of Canco was impoverishing itself to feed the starving strangers. The Canoandes Expedition was not yet halfway through the Colca Canyon and could go no farther.

Yet if their inspiration, John Paul II, could recover and carry on, so too must they. After inhaling a scant breakfast the next morning, Andrzej, Yurek, Piotr, and Jacek set out on the sixty-five-hundred-foot climb out of the canyon, with just their remaining one dollar and sixty-nine cents in their pockets. Somehow, they would have to rendezvous with Javier Ford, waiting with the truck in the regional capital, Arequipa, and then find the funds, food, and repair materials to reconstitute the expedition. They had estimated that two hungry Poles were the maximum the generous but poor seven families of Canco could feed, so Stefan and Biczu volunteered to remain with the equipment, on a diet of corn and occasional eggs, with no beer and no idea how long their teammates would be gone.

Just ten days later, a reconstituted Canoandes Expedition launched once again down the Colca. In that interval, they had managed to obtain funds from the loyal friends and supporters along their two-year, three-continent odyssey; order repair material from Lima; restock with food; obtain medical attention for Andrzej's infected eye; haul their supplies back down to Canco on muleback; and complete repairs of the torn raft floor and Piotr's decrepit kayak. Plus, the mule had brought Stefan and Biczu a few precious bottles of beer.

A major tributary joined from the right, and the Colca began to change in character. The flow had now increased to roughly seventeen hundred cubic feet per second, and it was noticeably warmer. Wider and more powerful rapids presented more open routes for the raft and kayak. The challenges were more those of traditional whitewater river running, less of rock climbing and portaging and lining the raft through congested rockfall sieves.* Their progress became swifter, the physical punishment and calorie drain of portaging reduced, but mile by mile the volume and power of the water increased, together with the whitewater risks. They celebrated stretches of easy, open passages that could be scouted from their boats, and they feared the big drops and the cliff walls that constrained stopping before blind corners.

Sometime during the third day below Canco they passed through the deepest part of the Colca Canyon. The scale was so great they could only sense the rims, lost behind towering steps and buttresses, soaring skyward 10,517 feet on their left, 13,696 feet on their right. In their imaginations the surrounding earth created an odd buoyancy, a gravity that pulled from all directions. Briefly, the river ceased its relentless gnawing into the earth and slid silently between the walls, as if it too were in awe of the majestic chasm it had created.

The walls ahead widened and rose, like a mad confectioner's fantasy, in tiers of every shade of brown and white: great whorls of lava like chocolate fudge, fine horizontal layers like ivory communion wafers, quartzite meringues, and latte icings. Igneous wedding cakes, Easter cakes, and tarts baked in the parched air. A beach of sun-warmed sand welcomed the paddlers, and for the moment the stresses and anxieties of the expedition seemed to melt away. As the sun retreated beyond the canyon's western rim, bats flickered in the gloaming, swift fragile life against the fairy-tale tableau. Yurek stood transfixed. *Oh God, please let us get out of this canyon so that we can tell the world about its beauty.*

Three days followed of ever bigger rapids that tested their nerve and skill and punished their slightest mistakes. They estimated they had

---

*In the final report published after the expedition, the team concluded that the section above Canco was a combination of paddling and mountaineering and was not recommended for navigation. The section below Canco they deemed navigable for expert paddlers and recommended highly. All subsequent expeditions have started at Hacienda Canco.

fourteen miles yet to run in the canyon when they used the last of their glue to repair a six-foot tear in the bottom of the raft. Piotr's kayak was held together only by duct tape and could no longer withstand the powerful drops. Yurek had lost his helmet days before. Again, their margin for error was razor thin. Halting to scout or carry became both more essential and more difficult in the bigger, pushier water. Krzysztof rode the bow of the raft, a steel piton tied to the mooring rope in one hand, a rock for a hammer in the other, ready to leap out at any opportunity and secure them to the shore.

They continued on, alternating risky runs and brutal carries, and, in the early afternoon of June 13, 1981, the canyon walls relented. The five rafters and Piotr in his kayak emerged to rolling hills and lush vegetation. A romp of otters appeared, sleek brown ghosts in turquoise water, coasting down the wave trains, magically reappearing in the eddies, playing hide-and-seek with the cameramen, escorting the clumsy raft and kayak down their final leg back to the world.

Javier arrived in the truck to transport them from the lunar wasteland of the canyon to the luxuries of Arequipa: red meat and cold beer; news of the world from television, radio, and newspapers; and a holy Catholic mass to give thanks for their protection and return. They bathed and weighed their emaciated bodies. Yurek had lost the most: 24 pounds. None had lost less than 15, and among the six explorers they had lost a total of 110 pounds of body weight.

Over the next six months they would recover their health; journey to their original objective, Argentina, to run the southernmost river on Earth (an anticlimactic several miles of flat water on the Rio Gallegos near Tierra del Fuego); and return to Lima to work on a book and film underwritten by the government of Peru.

And then, at dawn on December 13, 1981, came fate's final whiplash for the Canoandes '79 expedition. In Lima they had reveled in their celebrity as explorers and national heroes of Peru. The Peruvian

Ministry of Tourism scheduled a highly publicized launch for their book and film, to be attended by the president of Peru, Fernando Belaúnde Terry, in three days' time, on December 16. Their gear was packed out and already aboard a ship in anticipation of their scheduled triumphant return home to Poland on the twentieth — home with their families for Christmas!

All through the night of December 12, Yurek stood mesmerized on the floor of a print plant as the presses clattered out the initial copies of *In Kayak Through Peru: Whitewater Guide*, in Spanish and English. It was six o'clock the following morning before he walked back to their hotel through the waking streets of Lima, clutching the first copy of their collaborative book, wrapped in the satisfaction of yet another job well done, the cap to their three-year peregrination.

Even in his euphoria the breaking news of the day leaped out at him from a small newsstand: GOLPE EN POLONIA — MILITARES TOMAN EL PODER! [Coup in Poland — Military Takes Power!] In shock and disbelief, he struggled to steady his buckling knees. Their ultimate achievement, the exploration of the Colca Canyon, had begun with a vicious attack on their beloved pope. Was it now to end with the brutal suppression of their beloved country?

The sense of duty, to their nation and to their faith, that had impelled them through all the hard days in the Colca Canyon now led the Polish students to a higher cause — and greater risk. Capitalizing on their media status as the most visible Poles in Peru, they spearheaded protests against the martial law. On December 20, the day they had planned to fly home at last, they instead read an open letter to the president and people of Peru urging support for Solidarity at a sacred mass for Poland attended by three thousand people in Lima and broadcast live on national television. They organized, together with writer Mario Vargas Llosa and sculptor and painter Fernando de Szyszlo, a march of ten thousand protestors through the streets of Lima bearing posters of Lech Walesa and John Paul II.

Their protest activities were hugely popular in Lima, less so in Warsaw. A Polish diplomat still loyal to the overthrown government warned them to stay away from the Polish consulate for fear of possible arrest and forced repatriation. Others in Lima warned of the violent Peruvian Communist Party. But in yet another twist of luck, the visas that had previously gotten them to Casper, Wyoming, still had a few days before expiration, and a new friend at the American consulate cleared them to fly to New York, ostensibly "to run the Grand Canyon of the Colorado." The Canoandes Expedition was finally at an end after two and a half years, but the pilgrimage was far from over.*

---

*All obtained asylum in the West. Two settled in Canada, five (including photographer Zbigniew Bzdak, who missed the Colca Canyon because of malaria) in the United States. Not until the "fall of the wall" were they able to visit their families or to be recognized for their achievement in their homeland.

CHAPTER SEVEN

The Smoke That Thunders

The Zambezi River

> ...the most wonderful sight I had witnessed in Africa.
> — Dr. David Livingstone

Deborah Pratt had never been whitewater rafting before. It was logical, though, and reassuring, that everything would start with a safety briefing. She had also never been in Africa before, and what better place to start than iconic Victoria Falls, where the mile-wide Zambezi River leaps down more than three hundred feet into a crevasse of dark basalt and swirling water. She and her companion, LeVar Burton, filed eagerly into the meeting hall of the grand Edwardian hotel beside the falls in Zimbabwe to be prepared for their upcoming adventure. Life jackets, helmets, and raft guides' commands did not lead off the briefing, however. Instead, a government official flipped up a poster depicting a Claymore anti-personnel land mine, its oddly convex surface emblazoned THIS SIDE TOWARD ENEMY. In detail, he explained how much they wanted to avoid encountering one, its trip wires fine as fishing line, its C-4 plastic explosive propelling hundreds of flesh-tearing ball bearings. The same message accompanied pictures of black mamba snakes, then crocodiles, then baboons. Only at the end did a sandaled and deeply tanned raft guide discuss what to do if their raft overturned in the cauldron below.

After the briefing, Deborah and LeVar, the group's only two African American members, were asked to stay behind for a special ceremony. Their hosts slaughtered a goat and drank its blood to appease Nyami Nyami, a Zambezi water spirit with the body of a snake and the head of a fish.

Deborah was undeterred. She was young and adventurous, and, at a welcoming speech the following morning on the lip of the gorge, Zambia's president, Dr. Kenneth Kaunda, announced to one and all that this historic expedition was being undertaken by the most experienced river explorers in the world, veterans of more first descents on raging rivers than anyone — founder Richard Bangs and his world-famous Sobek Expeditions. Not only that, but an ABC film crew was here to record Sobek's exploit, as were photographers from *National Geographic* and a geographer from the University of Zambia. Adding Hollywood flair was Burton, the young Kunta Kinte in the wildly popular television epic *Roots*, here to celebrate his African heritage in a Sobek raft for the TV cameras. Sweeping his horsetail flyswatter in the air like a baton, President Kaunda climaxed his oration by leading the crowd in a full-throated chant of "One Sobek, One Zambia! One Sobek, One Zambia!" Deborah figured she was with the A-team.

President Kaunda in fact knew no more about river rafting than did Deborah. In desperation the night before this opening ceremony, his aides had asked Richard Bangs if he could please write some appropriate remarks for the president. Richard had been only too happy to comply. His nerve on big rivers was at least matched by his audacity in promoting his rafting company. This was his moment. He was here in the footsteps of Livingstone, and he had brought his circus with him.

Dr. Livingstone, the Scottish explorer, had abandoned his attempt to descend the Zambezi at Victoria Falls in 1855, and by the 1970s, as expedition whitewater, by kayak and by raft, developed enough to even attempt the run, the Zambezi was central to a vicious decade of guerrilla warfare. Beginning in 1966, from bases in Zambia, along the river corridor and its tributary side canyons, rebels of the Zimbabwe African National Union raided into Rhodesia to bring down its white-minority government. Rhodesian security forces responded in deadly kind, a ruthless war of raid and ambush, of anti-personnel mines and booby traps, where no man could tread safely.

The armed struggle ended late in 1980, brokered by British prime minister Margaret Thatcher, and the majority-rule nation of Zimbabwe emerged from the ashes of Rhodesia. Eager to resume tourist income from their greatest natural resource, Zambia on the north and Zimbabwe to the south hosted a group of international tour operators at Victoria Falls in February 1981 to announce that, with peace, they were reopening for business. They had prioritized clearing the land mines from trails and overlooks. In the depths of the gorge below, who but the crocodiles would care?

The tour operators gazed upstream at one of the grandest sights in nature, at thousands of tons of water roaring over the wide lip into the narrow gorge below, forcing sun-bright columns of mist hundreds of feet upward into the air. Mosi-oa-Tunya, this place was called, the Smoke That Thunders.* His back to the others, Hatch River Expeditions protégé Richard Bangs stared downstream at dark rock, lime-green water, two feather-white rapids. Until just months ago, this river had been forbidden to the world for more than a decade. It had never been attempted; now two governments were eager to support travel opportunities. The whole world was celebrating the end of colonialism in Africa. With the right publicity, prospects of a tourist rafting concession could be immeasurable. Anything looks runnable from 350 feet above.

Eight months later, after President Kaunda's stirring address, the 1981 Great Zambezi Expedition paraded down a steep trail on the Zambian bank to the Boiling Pot, a giant swirling eddy below the base of the falls. Six gray, sixteen-foot Avon rafts with yellow stripes, SOBEK in red and yellow foot-high letters emblazoned on their pneumatic tubes,

---

* Mosi-oa-Tunya / Victoria Falls was designated a UNESCO World Heritage Site in 1989.

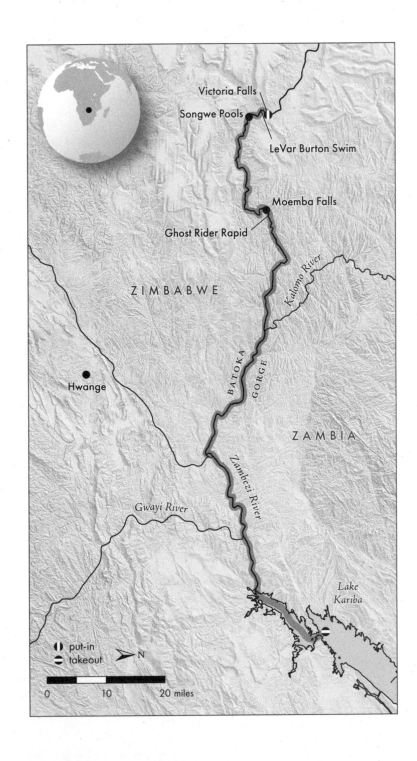

were followed by two bright plastic kayaks for safety boaters Neusom Holmes and Doug Tompkins.* Raft guides John Yost, Skip Horner, Jim Slade, Dave Shore, John Kramer, and ringmaster Bangs scrambled to the rocks at river's edge with celebrities LeVar Burton and Deborah Pratt, photographer Nick Nichols, historian and pioneer rafter Grant Rogers, geographer Dennis Huckabay from the University of Zambia, and a gaggle of excited local boys.

Producer John Wilcox and his film crew from ABC's *American Sportsman* TV series positioned themselves along the trail, across the river, and high on the bridge above.

Not to be outdone by the president of Zambia, an olive-drab-and-tan-camouflaged helicopter from the Zimbabwean army chattered importantly overhead: an aerial scout, a shuttle to insert army sappers to sweep campsites for mines, and a medevac if required. A second helicopter, hired by the film crew as a camera platform, hovered. Just twelve months before, any helicopters in the area would have been there to insert camouflage-painted night raiders.

Richard smiled reassuringly to his two apprehensive passengers, settled firmly into his rowing seat, and let the raft drift, gently at first, up toward the head of the surging Boiling Pot eddy. As they approached the upstream point, he set his oars and drove powerfully forward, out into the crashing downstream current of fifteen thousand cubic feet per second. His next stroke would set them firmly on their way downstream. Instead, in the surging waves one blade planted securely in the water, but the other grabbed nothing but air. The raft swung drunkenly and was dashed into a wall of whitewater and black basalt. Richard tried in vain to regain control, Nick Nichols continued shooting photos, someone screamed, and the raft, pushed vertically up beyond its balance point, spilled its passengers and flipped. Observing from the

---

* Doug Tompkins founded the North Face in 1964. He would later devote his life and fortune to acquiring more than two million acres of mountain and river wilderness across Chile and Argentina, which he then donated to become national parks. He died of hypothermia in a kayaking accident in southern Chile in 2015; his widow, Kris Tompkins, continues this extraordinary conservation legacy.

bridge high above, President Kaunda asked, of no one in particular, "Is that how they do it?"

Even before the swamped raft was reunited with its bedraggled former occupants, the guides by consensus named that rapid "Riches to Rags."

The other boats made it out of the gigantic eddy without mishap, and the expedition left behind its throngs of observers, the unfamiliar raft teams gradually getting their sea legs. All but one of the rafts were oar rigs, rowed by a single guide — the preferred method for professional rafting on big, difficult rivers. One was paddled by all its occupants, which included experienced guide Dave Shore, sixty-six-year-old veteran rafter Grant Rogers, and first-timer LeVar Burton, in order to place the actor at the heart of ABC's story line as an active participant in the adventure. At three more big rapids the Sobek guides had to reappraise opinions they'd formed during aerial reconnaissance. The ones that had appeared the worst offered straightforward lines, while others presented nasty surprises. They managed to run them all with no further flips or swims, although the paddled raft team opted for discretion and portaged around the last rapid of the day.

The helicopter that had stalked them all day swooped in to extract the ABC film crew back to the rim-side hotel, where Wilcox would work deep into the night reviewing the day's takes, conferring with his crew on the story line and shots planned for the next day on the river.

As the subtropical night swiftly enveloped the riverside camp, a swath of unfamiliar Southern Hemisphere stars, implausibly bright in the unpolluted African sky and framed by shadow-black canyon walls, illuminated the beach. The guides were a silent, introspective group this first night, each consumed by deeply familiar but inexpressible feelings: that sublime contentment they found nowhere but on wild rivers and the adrenaline anticipation of risks downstream: at once in their true home and deep in the heart of Africa on a stretch of river no one had ever attempted.

In all the wonderful diversity of Africa, no place has better claim to be its heart. In its sixteen-hundred-mile course across the southern part of the continent, the Zambezi River flows neither around great mountain chains, as do the Indus and the Tsangpo, nor through them like the Inn and the Kali Gandaki. It flows across great, horizontal sheets of extruded volcanic basalt, hundreds of feet thick. Where it cascades off the rim, the spectacular falls that drew Richard Bangs, which were "discovered" by David Livingstone and named for the British queen to become the symbol of British imperialism in Africa, are in geologic fact but the eighth and most recent incarnation of a natural wonder that has been marching upstream in gigantic steps across 150 million years of African history.

The slightest fissure in the hard lip of the falls allows hydraulic forces to concentrate, speeding erosion in an inevitable cycle that, over eons, cuts another gorge and leaves another waterfall to spill over another rim upstream. As the rafters made their first camp below Victoria Falls, the Devils Cataract on its western end was already more than one hundred feet lower than the rest of the falls, the mile-wide curtain of water already doomed to become a single slot.

Human prehistory too runs old and deep along the Zambezi. Cave paintings date back hundreds of thousands of years, and an unbroken archaeological record traces back, culture upon culture upon culture, all the way to stone hand tools ascribed to the Oldowan industry, the earliest known human artifacts. A million years of the evolution of man hung in the campfire smoke.

There was little time for introspection in the morning, when the television group choppered in for the second act. Immediately downstream from camp, the fifth major rapid of the run promised to be the most difficult yet. In their study of aerial photographs, and their helicopter scout courtesy of the Zimbabwean military, they had judged this to be a portage. But in the invigorating morning light, from river level, it offered a clean line down the right-hand side — if only a gigantic, washed-over rock obstructing the entrance could be avoided.

Guide John Kramer showed the way in one of the oar rigs, threading the needle to the right of the entrance pour-over and the nasty hole behind it. The two safety kayaks followed without incident, then the remaining oar rigs.

Upon the signal that cameras were at the ready, Dave Shore eased his paddle raft into the current above, calling commands to his crew of LeVar Burton and historian Grant Rogers to ferry across to the narrow entrance slot above the drop. Unaccountably, the paddlers lost their rhythm, and with it their momentum. The raft wallowed over the pour-over rock and into the hole behind it. Bucking wildly, it launched Burton and Rogers into the river, then escaped the hole and washed downstream, alternately in front of, on top of, and behind the swimmers. Rescue kayaker Neusom Holmes shot out and quickly pulled LeVar to shore, legs skinned up but otherwise unharmed, before the avid TV cameras.

Sixty-six-year-old Grant Rogers was not so lucky. He washed over a small waterfall, recirculated in the backwash below, and was ejected out into the main current with a collapsed lung and four broken ribs. It was doubtful he could have held the end of a kayak to be towed to safety, but Bangs and Yost chased him down in one of the rafts and rolled him painfully aboard. The army helicopter was a French-made Alouette, long a workhorse for mountain rescue in the Alps. Now it proved its heritage, swooping in to evacuate Rogers to the nearest hospital, eighty miles away, where he was stabilized and dispatched back stateside for a full recovery. Watching the camouflaged helicopter disappear over the canyon rim, the wind and roar of its rotors fading, replaced by the surging of the river, those left behind were starkly reminded that the Zambezi was neither big top nor soundstage, and Nyami Nyami would not be storyboarded.

Three easy rapids followed, lime-green water, lush dripping vegetation, a soaring African fish eagle. Then the bottom fell out. The width of the river narrowed to a single chute and disappeared from the rafters' view. Scrambling down the shoreline, they gazed down into a single, grinding hole — impossible to tell how deep — followed by a tower of white that would dwarf a sixteen-foot raft. Most agreed it was the largest rapid they had ever seen. Without discussion they unloaded their gear and began the awkward labor of wrestling the bulky inflatables along the steep, rocky bank.

They made a camp that second night at Songwe Pools, a large, slick eddy and a sand beach formed where a side canyon joined the river from the left, a welcome oasis from a world of jagged rock. In the unaccustomed silence, the river whispered and hissed against the rocky shore, with an occasional ghostly *plock* or splash caused by random turbulence or unknown creature.

From the first day, when he eagerly pitched in to learn his part in paddling the raft, and the first night, when he insisted on camping with the rafters in the gorge rather than retreating back to the hotel with the film crew, LeVar Burton had steadily grown in the eyes of the raft guides. As professional guides, they had a cowboy attitude toward the rich, the entitled, and the famous. Only actions counted. In the *American Sportsman* television series, ABC's formula was to depict a well-known celebrity on an outdoor adventure, believing that a general audience would be better drawn into the story. In this case the celebrity needed to be a Black American, since part of ABC's story line was that person connecting with their African ancestry, and they needed to be engaging, and tough enough to go down the river.

The raft guides would have preferred a famous athlete to a Hollywood actor. As John Wilcox and Richard Bangs began their planning, middleweight fighter Sugar Ray Leonard seemed the obvious first choice, and the young guides were thrilled at the thought of introducing the hero of the boxing ring to their world. They had heard, however, that there was a catch. Sugar Ray was to fight Thomas Hearns for the World Welterweight Championship in Las Vegas on September 16, 1981, little more than a month before the Zambezi expedition and filming. If he lost, the river trip would be a much-needed training break and recuperation period, but if he won, he would be a multimillion-dollar property in too much demand to disappear into Africa. At the Sobek headquarters in Angel Camp, California, and at riverbank camps around the world, the Thomas Hearns rooting section groaned in unison as Sugar Ray staggered Hearns with an overhand right in the fourteenth round and won the title by TKO. *ABC's Wide World of Sports* named Sugar Ray Athlete of the Year, and *American Sportsman* had to turn elsewhere for its hero.

On the river, they soon learned that LeVar too had athletic talent, and his unfazed attitude about his swim and banged-up legs that morning impressed the guides. And in those campfire evenings, among tales of humor, adventure, and disaster around the globe, he was not without stories of his own. In the iconic miniseries *Roots*, LeVar played the young hero, and in an early scene set in Africa, former NFL running back O. J. Simpson was the father of a young Mandinkan maiden. An irate O. J. was to pursue and berate LeVar for upsetting his daughter's meal preparation as he chased a guinea fowl through camp. On the set, the younger and smaller LeVar, a former track and field competitor, exceeded all expectations in portraying a fleeing youth. What started as acting out a flight in terror became a game and then a taunt, until the director had to order LeVar to stop horsing around and let O. J. seize him as scripted. Back at the campfire, LeVar's rapt audience mulled over how toe-to-toe with Thomas Hearns stacked up to toe-to-toe with O. J. Simpson.

An exhilarating day followed, with great trains of standing waves, roller-coaster rides without penalty, then smooth, silent intervals gliding downstream. Deborah Pratt drifted, mesmerized by the swift, serpentine river: the light changing at every bend, alternating from inky black reflection of the canyon walls to translucent shades of green, swirls deep below the surface like muscles rippling beneath the watery skin; its capricious moods, from nurturing bearer-of-life to roaring, white-maned dragon. On either side, sturdy rock shoulders jutted hundreds of feet upward, the Jurassic bedrock of Africa itself, enfolding and defending its river. Deborah reflected on how far away she was from the canyons of Chicago where she'd grown up.*

As the others disembarked and began to make camp late that afternoon, Neusom, relieved of his rescue responsibilities, surfed and played in his kayak on a set of waves just upstream, an intimate dance with the flow of water and the pull of gravity, from waltz to tango depending on the river's whim. As he shot across the faces of the waves, adjusting the twist of his hips and the lean of his body to carve exhilarating arcs in the swift current, he was suddenly aware of another presence with him, a dark form barely glimpsed in the turbulence. Spooked, he spun his bow downstream and paddled to rejoin the others on shore.

Even before that memorable safety briefing, there had been talk and speculation about the crocodiles known to be abundant downstream. But this, concluded both the locals and the old pros from Ethiopia, Bangs and Yost, must have been just a floating log in the uncertain light. Here in the swift clear water, between steep rocky banks, they were too far upstream to worry about crocodiles, which preferred the long, turgid pools and muddy banks they would find farther down the river. Neusom was unconvinced. He had seen a log with a head three feet long.

Just as Mike Jones and Leo Dickinson knew on Everest, John Wilcox was aware that if dramatic events were not captured on film, in frame and in focus, then for mass audiences they might as well have never happened. Campfire stories might titillate the small brotherhood of river runners; they would not satisfy the ABC viewership. Wilcox had the advantages of a large budget, professional crew, and helicopter platform, and the corresponding pressure to produce. However, the first descent of a huge unknown river is just that, a huge unknown. Events devolve from routine to emergency in split seconds. Wildlife

* Seven years later she would journey farther yet — in time and space — as co-creator and executive producer of the iconic science-fiction TV series *Quantum Leap*.

appears and disappears to no man's schedule. And unlike the nimble Czech and British kayakers on the Dudh Kosi, no one was going to spend hours lugging the rafts back upstream on foot to provide multiple takes. Each night he reviewed the day's film and made decisions for the morrow.

The following day was to be, Wilcox now determined, the last on the river for LeVar and Deborah. Both were thrilled with the rafting and the African adventure, but keeping a Hollywood actor and producer in the field, and a full-time helicopter in the air, was enormously expensive, and he was now confident he had all the footage of LeVar that he needed. The abrupt end to LeVar's quest for his African roots halfway down the run would go unnoticed in the film. During their lunch break that last day, LeVar finally had some free time to get in Doug Tompkins's kayak for an introductory lesson from Holmes. Having intently observed Neusom for the past several days, he was soon darting around the small riffle by their beach with aplomb. All too soon, though, the rafts began reloading, and LeVar and Neusom reluctantly broke off the lesson to rejoin the procession downstream.

In the first riffle, still within sight of the luncheon beach, a fury of leathery scales and yellowed teeth lunged from below John Yost's raft, seizing and exploding one of its inflated chambers. Wielding an oar and balancing from long practice on the slippery undulating rubber floor of the raft, Yost bashed the croc's snout repeatedly. It made one more lunge, then sank from sight as abruptly as it had appeared. Hastily reseating his oar, Yost pulled the deflating raft, and wide-eyed photographer Nick Nichols, to shore, where they were quickly joined by the other rafts and the two safety kayaks. Estimates of the size of the attacker ranged from nine to twelve feet. What such a surprise attack would have done to a kayaker was unthinkable.

Previously in Ethiopia, Bangs and Yost had observed, as Mike Jones and Mick Hopkinson had done before them, that crocodiles tended to surface in the muddy water to observe their objectives from some distance before a final approach, and they could often be avoided or driven off by gunfire, rocks, or even noise. This sudden, untelegraphed assault from below, perhaps the result of the clearer and swifter water, was as unexpected as it was unnerving.

In a flurry of radio calls, Wilcox recalled his film crew, Burton, and Pratt to the hotel on the rim above. The incoming helicopter rent the afternoon quiet with a roar and a cyclone of rotor-wash sand, and in the scurry of off-loading supplies for the rafters, uploading passengers and outgoing equipment (which now included the fatally wounded raft and both bite-sized kayaks), LeVar and Deborah barely had time to say good-bye.

Richard Bangs rowed downstream the following day with a much smaller and more elemental expedition. Kayakers Holmes and Tompkins joined the others in the rafts. The six-hundred-foot walls widened a bit and, fringed by a rim of mopane trees, framed a pristine African sky — twists of white cirrus gleaming in a field of blue above the green-and-white river. Ahead were unknown rapids to be run, falls to be portaged, and crocodiles. Behind, all the other layers: the officialdom of two countries, the needs and obligations of filming, the Hollywood story line superimposed onto their adventure. The circus had left town.

Moemba Falls was a known, pre-planned portage, and an awesome sight when seen up close, even for these experienced river runners. Compressed to a width of fifty or sixty feet, the entire Zambezi plunged twenty feet down into an enormous hole "that seems, in its impact, to tear the grim basaltic rocks asunder," wrote explorer G. W. Lamplugh in 1905. The team could feel its deep subsonic percussion through the air around them and the rock under their feet. Not far downstream they encountered a second falls, unnamed, unknown, and unexpected. It was less impressive to look at, but the carry around was difficult, and through the long afternoon they struggled along a steep and broken shore, each of the five rafts a four-man carry. Everything had to be lowered down a short cliff, and it was late in the day before they had the rafts reloaded and could resume the descent.

Daylight was fading, and Richard estimated they had about three miles yet to cover before their planned campsite, when the roar and the horizon line of a big rapid appeared ahead. After a hasty scout they determined to run it through a set of huge exploding waves down the center. Seated at the oars of his raft in the eddy above, Richard watched Neusom Holmes row down the centerline, rise cleanly over the first wave, emerge sideways from the trough, and flip on the exploding second wave, ejecting him and his passengers into the gathering dark below. Racing to help, Skip Horner narrowly slipped over that second wave and, Richard assumed, made it safely down. Jim Slade and his passengers followed, and like Holmes they capsized on the second wave, then disappeared from Richard's view.

Two flips in the same rapid had not happened to them before on the Zambezi — not even close. They were rushing to find camp at the end of a long and exhausting day. Richard had no idea how those downstream had fared; he could only hope that Skip Horner was down there sorting out the swimmers.

He was. Racing the gathering darkness, and with that afternoon's croc attack foremost in the minds of rescuers and swimmers alike, Skip and his crew recovered the two swamped rafts and desperately sought to account for the occupants. The head count was one short; a swimmer had wound up, unobserved, in an eddy above. In what he describes as "the scariest thirty seconds" of his adventurous life, it fell to Dave Shore to dive into the inky water to be sure the missing man was not trapped underneath a raft, as Bus Hatch had been on the Indus. It was at once terrifying and what these professional guides lived for: taking disaster and making it right again.

Upstream, Richard desperately looked for an easier "sneak route" down one side or the other, but it was already too dark to tell. On impulse, he strapped down his oars inside the raft, grabbed his diary and camera, stepped ashore, and pushed the empty raft into the current. In the gloaming, he watched the yellow-striped craft accelerate in the main stream, line up a bit left of where the previous runners had gone, and plunge into the rapid with no one at the oars — except, perhaps, Nyami Nyami.

The rafters gathered below stared upstream, trying to make out the reason for delay. After long minutes they finally could make out the raft lumbering over the first wave and disappearing into the trough. Only when it rose cleanly up and over the second wave could they see that the apparition contained no human occupant. They had barely shepherded the loose raft in to shore when its former master arrived, stumbling down the dark shoreline. This, then, by accident or design, was expedition rafting stripped down all the way. No cameras, no observers, not even any light. No ringleader, no actors, not even a guide at the oars. Just the river, and the raft, and whatever sent it down that clean line. They named this rapid Ghost Rider.

CHAPTER EIGHT

Tiger Leaping

The Yangtze River

See you on the other side.

— Lei Jiansheng and Li Qinjian,
putting in above Tiger Leaping Gorge

Along with its annual floods and tons of sediment, the Yangtze River carries the soul of the ancient Chinese nation: its rice-growing agriculture; its inland commerce; the merging currents of Buddha, Confucius, and Lao-tzu; the still-vivid epic of Mao's Long March. Fifteen hundred miles downstream from its source in Tibet, in the words of author Simon Winchester, "the great ragged ranges of Sichuan and Yunnan, the granite and limestone temple guardians of Tibet," close in on the mighty river. For twelve miles, tens of thousands of cubic feet of water per second pulse and thunder more than six hundred vertical feet down huge ledges. By legend a tiger fleeing hunters leaped to safety across this maelstrom, so narrow is the constriction. In the 1980s, winds of change roiling Chinese society funneled to hurricane force in the canyons of the Yangtze and came to a crescendo in Tiger Leaping Gorge.*

Evening, September 8, 1986, Yunnan Province, China
Virtually every member of the independent Luoyang Rafting Team clamored to be selected to attempt the Upper Tiger Leaping Gorge.

---

* Tiger Leaping Gorge (Hutiao Xia) on the Yangtze and parallel sections of the Mekong and Salween Rivers were designated a UNESCO World Heritage Site, the Yunnan Protected Areas, in 2003.

The leaders and veterans who had been with the team from the beginning caucused, then emerged to announce their decision. Lei Jiansheng and Li Qinjian withdrew, sobbing with pride and fear, to write final letters to their families in case they did not survive.

All resemblance to rafting or river running — and perhaps to sport — as understood in the West had gradually disappeared as the team made its way along the fifteen-hundred-mile course of the Yangtze from the highlands of Tibet. As the river grew more and more powerful, they had abandoned all attempts at steering their rafts, instead creating completely enclosed capsules into which the occupants were strapped with breathing devices, to be pushed out into the current and recovered from downstream eddies by shore teams. Two members of their team had already drowned in a prototype device upstream. Now their newest capsule had dramatically failed one of its few tests. It had been torn open in its only time on the water and required makeshift repairs.

Team leader Maojun Wang swallowed his doubts. He suggested that just a single man occupy the capsule so that if the run were fatal only one man would die instead of two, but his comrades would have none of it. As soon as Lei Jiansheng and Li Qinjian were selected to run the first part of the gorge, the others began arguing furiously for selection to attempt the middle segment.

The frenetic discussion continued into the night at a rock quarry / reeducation camp in Lijiang City, when, shortly after midnight, a convoy of vehicles pulled up to the Luoyang Team base, headlights glistening in a cold rain, tires spitting wet clay and marble dust. Director Hou Huiren, commander in chief of the rival Sichuan Scientific Drift Team, emerged with a host of staff and media. He and team leader Wang tried to adjourn to a private space, but members of both teams packed into the room reeking of kerosene smoke, damp wool, and sweaty bodies. The grizzled old cadreman, comrade of Mao through World War II and the Long March, now in his sixties and almost twice Wang's age, tapped his cane for emphasis and came right to the point. "Old Wang,* are you guys actually going for Upper Tiger Leaping Gorge tomorrow?"

"Yes sir," Wang responded, with equal courtesy and resolve.

Director Hou tried first to order, then to cajole, the Luoyang Team into delaying their attempt. The risks were huge. The honor of the Chinese nation would be diminished if they were to fail. His much larger and better equipped Sichuan Team had just arrived that day, and together they could put together a much stronger attempt.

Speaking as much to the members of his own team packed into the corners of the room as he was to Director Hou, Wang rebutted. Of course the risks were great. That was the nature of adventure, the reason they were all here. They would be equally great in a week, or a month. And the honor of the nation rested with Director Hou, not with Luoyang. The Sichuan Team was the expedition officially sanctioned and supported by the government of Sichuan Province, publicized with great fanfare by the Chinese media. Wang's Luoyang Team were no more than individual citizens, self-supported, representing no one, beholden to no one, even opposed by officials at times. Should they fail, it would be of no import. Besides, he added, hoping to end the argument, it was too late. The press had been notified and teams dispatched to recover the capsule below the upper gorge.

Director Hou was not dissuaded. "That's easy. Notify your teams tomorrow to pull off; as for the media, just make another announcement."

Even had he wanted to, acceding to a delay now would not be possible for Wang. His leadership was not autocratic, not by appointment from any official authority or agency. He was recognized as leader by the idiosyncratic members of the Luoyang Team for his vision, his determination, and his powers of persuasion. Lei Jiansheng and Li Qinjian were now in isolation, their psyches screwed up to near-suicidal levels. The rest of the team were not far behind. And all, not least Wang, harbored deep resentments against Director Hou

---

* The honorific *old* before his name is used here to indicate affinity or familiarity.

and the Sichuan Team that had been building over the months the two teams had leapfrogged down the upper river. When their rivals were stalled and awaiting replacement equipment, Wang had loaned them rafts, three of which were lost or damaged. That cooperation was not reciprocated when his own team needed help. And the much larger and better-equipped "official" team had dominated the growing Chinese media spotlight on this unprecedented descent, galling the egos of the members of the Luoyang Team and hindering their already limited fundraising. If Wang were to try to force a delay now, his team members would listen to other, more radical voices. They might never recover their present degree of cohesion and resolve.

Unspoken, but also looming in the minds of all in that heated midnight conference, was a formidable third rival seeking to claim the mantle of first to descend the Yangtze River. From the vast desolation of the Tibetan frontier, both teams heard little news. They knew only that Beijing had shamefully sold to foreigners the right to first navigate the length of their national river; that a world-famous American river rafter and his team had arrived in China that summer with nine tons of the most modern equipment; that the Americans had trained for years to claim this prize their own; and that they were now somewhere upstream, in silent pursuit.

The attempt of Upper Tiger Leaping Gorge would launch that day.

Sport — initially the unlikely sport of Ping-Pong — had proved to be the basis for China's first, tentative outreach to the world as the chaos and cruelty of Mao Zedong's Cultural Revolution wound down in the early 1970s. As a result of its long, "Bamboo Curtain" isolation, the Chinese economy was desperate for hard currency. The United States was almost equally eager to put their Vietnam experience behind and reengage with the rest of the Pacific community of nations. Sport as a tool of state power and propaganda was integral to communist doctrine, even more so in China than in Czechoslovakia and Poland.

A chance encounter between Chinese and American competitors at a Ping-Pong tournament in Japan in April 1971 led to a formal invitation for a US team to visit — a precursor to visits soon after by then National Security Advisor Henry Kissinger and President Richard Nixon to crack open the doors, not just of sport, but of trade and diplomacy as well.

In America, Ping-Pong was widely regarded as mere rec-room entertainment. The Chinese Ping-Pong team, however, was a powerhouse in international competition, could walk with pride on the world stage, and was a natural to lead the way for an entire nation. With their huge population base and cultural willingness to go all-in to achieve their ends, China's athletes would soon move into the top ranks of a variety of Olympic sports.

In the outdoor sports, however, East met West in curious fashion. The Chinese had little tradition of climbing, or even trekking, and zero of whitewater river running. Geographically, however, they were home to some of the greatest unclaimed prizes in the world of exploration and adventure. While China cut itself off from the outside world for most of the twentieth century due to civil war, world war, and communist xenophobia, the greatest Himalayan peaks outside of China had, one by one, been climbed. The highest peak in the world yet unclimbed was the southeastern anchor of the Himalayas, Mount Namcha Barwa, looming to 25,251 feet in Tibet.* Great rivers had been explored in Africa, Asia, and North and South America. The two greatest prizes yet to be attempted both flowed out of Tibet: The Tsangpo looped around Mount Namcha Barwa, to become the Brahmaputra of India; and the Yangtze descended through Yunnan to define the heart of China itself.

The first hint of opening during the Ping-Pong diplomacy kindled the dreams of adventurers worldwide. From Seattle, American climber Jim Wickwire queried about Namcha Barwa. A permit could

---

* Successfully climbed by a joint Japanese/Chinese team in 1992, the culmination of three years of attempts.

be arranged, replied Beijing, for a million dollars. From Angel Camp, California, Richard Bangs's Sobek rafting inquired about the Yangtze. It too was possible, for a million dollars. River rafter and backpacker Bruce Berkman from Los Angeles proposed the Tsangpo. For a mere ten thousand dollars he could travel into Tibet to scout; the permit itself would then be a million. Japanese, West Germans, New Zealanders, and others inquired as well — each hoping to keep their plans secret and to avoid a bidding war. The communist functionaries in Beijing, however, had a firm grasp on the supply and demand curves of their mountains and rivers.

Contrary to some Western preconceptions, though, China was just too big and too complex to be governed simply by fiat from the top. There was a contradictory crosscurrent in China, a fervent nationalism and spirit of self-determination taking hold as a new generation sought its identity after the throes of the Cultural Revolution. One manifestation was a general suspicion of and resistance to the dictates of far-off bureaucrats in Beijing, another an insistence that native Chinese be the first to claim the great adventure sports prizes within their country, regardless of the fact that China had neither the traditions, skills, nor equipment to mount major expeditions.

In 1985, after seven years of dreaming, planning, and promoting, Oregon rafter Ken Warren broke the code and scored the prized permit to run the length of the Yangtze from its glacial origin to the head of commercial navigation — 1,973 unexplored miles dropping nearly 17,000 feet — the following year. In addition to rafting clients down Oregon's Snake, Deschutes, Owyhee, and Rogue Rivers, he had twice participated in whitewater rafting expeditions to the headwaters of the Ganges in the Indian Himalayas led by Everest climber Lute Jerstad. Ever since, Warren had been obsessed with leading his own expedition — on what he proclaimed, with considerable justification, the one great unrun river left in the world: the Yangtze. His winning formula was twofold.

Jerstad's second Himalayan rafting expedition, on the Alakananda in 1977, was filmed by ABC Television's *American Sportsman*, making Warren a known figure to the American television public and to producer John Wilcox. With his lanky frame, sun-bronzed face, and carefully groomed shock of blond hair going gray at his temples, the fifty-nine-year-old hunter, fisherman, packhorse guide, and rafting outfitter was the perfect image of an American outdoorsman. He and his wife, Jan, who would manage logistics for the expedition, were attractive, articulate, and obsessed — ideal subjects for Wilcox's lens.

Collaboration came at a good time for both men. ABC had recently wound down its long-running *American Sportsman* show, which had been influential in the growth of expedition whitewater for more than a decade: Rob Lesser's first run on the Stikine, Richard Bangs's first run on the Zambezi, Walt Blackadar on Turnback Canyon of the Alsek, and countless others. Wilcox was launching a new television partnership with *Mutual of Omaha's Spirit of Adventure*, a spin-off adding an element of outdoor adventure to the acclaimed nature series *Wild Kingdom*. Without accurate maps, and without any support by land or air between road access points often hundreds of unknown river miles apart, Warren's plans for the Yangtze would be on a scale beyond the Indus, the Dudh Kosi, or the Zambezi. In Wilcox's words, "Exploration with a capital E."

Mutual of Omaha's filming budget was a major contribution to Ken Warren's overall expedition funding, and Wilcox's TV imprimatur would influence both the Chinese and other potential sponsors. But they were still far short of the Chinese million-dollar ask. What Warren proposed next was to be good television and even better politics. In the year before the expedition, he would fly three Chinese-selected athletes to Oregon and train them as river rafters at his outfitting company. They would become the nucleus of a Sino-USA Upper Yangtze River Expedition. Even as translator Chu Siming, canoeing instructor and coach for the Chinese Olympic rowing team

Xu Jusheng, and mountaineer Zhang Jiyue developed their river skills on the Rogue, the Salmon, and Hell's Canyon of the Snake, negotiations continued over the price of the permit. The million dropped to $700,000, then to $325,000 — and the dream became reality. Launch was set for the summer of 1986.

But the race down the Yangtze had already begun a year earlier. In remote Sichuan, Yao Maoshu had dreamed of rafting the Yangtze almost as long as Warren. As a university student the notion of rafting the entire length of the river first captured his imagination, fueling dreams of glory as an explorer and acclaim as a photographer. For seven years he researched the river, observed different sections, floated smaller rivers with hand-me-down rafts and equipment from university programs. And then his application to participate on the Sino-American expedition was rejected by the China Sports Service in Beijing. Far from discouraging Yao Maoshu, this rejection hardened his resolve to accomplish his dream, to do it immediately, and to do it alone as now seemed necessary. He hastily acquired a twelve-foot lifeboat-style raft, which he named *Dragon's Descendant*; cameras and film; and rudimentary waterproof clothing and camping gear.

He launched in mid-June 1985, from the foot of Mount Geladandong, the official source of the Yangtze, and for six hundred miles he drifted alone through the labyrinthine braided channels and glacial debris islands of the upper river. Bears and wolves threatened his campsites, but the river presented little more than riffles. He arrived at the first town, Yushu, starving for both food and human company. There he restocked on supplies donated by town officials, and he left his exposed film, his journals to date, and letters to his family with a local news reporter for forwarding.

Yao Maoshu set off downstream on July 23, 1985. The following day herdsmen eighteen miles downstream discovered his body awash in an eddy, unrecoverable on the far side of the river, just below a short canyon with several moderate rapids. As the story rippled out from remote Yushu, his quixotic journey and lonely death transfixed the nation. From his surviving journals, letters, and interviews with the reporter in Yushu, Yao Maoshu's sentiment to risk all for China's national honor, and his refusal to accept the three Chinese who had been selected for the Sino-USA Expedition as more than tokens, spread widely among youth and academic circles.

Dreamers, adventurers, and fervent nationalists throughout China began concocting plans to complete Yao Maoshu's quest to descend the entire length of the Yangtze before the American expedition, and in the middle of June 1986, within days of each other, two rival expeditions actually launched. They were as different from each other as they were from their foreign nemesis.

To the displeasure of the China Sports Service in Beijing, the Institute of Geographical Research, a branch of the Chinese Academy of Sciences located in Chengdu, the capital of Sichuan Province through which the Yangtze flows, organized the China Yangtze River Scientific Observation Drifting Expedition (Sichuan Scientific Drift Team). Into their original team they incorporated participants from ten provinces and five ethnic minorities, thus laying claim to both official sanction and national representation. Their stated objectives were not only to run the river but also to collect geographic, geologic, and anthropological data along the way.* The group was large (forty-eight total on the original team), relatively well funded and equipped (about sixty thousand dollars with a dozen old but serviceable rafts), and organized in military fashion.

From the industrial city of Luoyang in central China, idealistic young workers, independent of any governmental or media backing and on a shoestring budget, pulled together the Luoyang Expedition for Sailing and Exploring the Yangtze (Luoyang Team): eight men to

---

* A throwback, perhaps, to a more nineteenth-century philosophy of exploring and mountaineering with at least a veneer of field science.

start, with an initial fund of six thousand dollars and two lightweight fourteen-foot paddle rafts. They had but one goal: to run the Yangtze before the Sino-USA Expedition and the Sichuan Scientific Team.

The rival Chinese expeditions did share two things in common: zero whitewater rafting experience and a curious "code of honor," which dictated that to run the river successfully, every single rapid must be survived by at least one person. Once that was accomplished, by whatever means, the whole expedition could proceed to the next obstacle.

1124 hours, September 9, 1986, Yunnan Province, China
"See you on the other side." Lei Jiansheng and Li Qinjian embraced the two teammates who would seal them into the black rubberized capsule, studded with truck inner tubes for extra flotation, and push them out into the unknown.

News reporters and film crews packed a rocky beach on the left shore, below the largest of the upper drops, where a huge pyramid of wet-black limestone (across which the legendary tiger leaped) split the gray flood, flanked by colossal recirculating holes. Opposite, the clinging vegetation curled back, and upended planes of limestone plunged like fangs into the Yangtze. Prison laborers from the rock quarry, and their armed guards, dotted the shoreline as well, to watch this patriotic and inspirational deed that had been deemed reeducational. Despite their contretemps in the early-morning hours, the Sichuan Team turned out to support with manpower, extra radios, and medical treatment if required.

The first retrieval team stood by to catch the ungainly vessel if it washed into an eddy on their side or to report its progress to teams downstream if it were swept past. A second team was positioned with the media and other observers where a large recirculating eddy marked the end of the upper gorge, and a third between the middle and lower gorges. All were confined to the left bank. There was no access to the

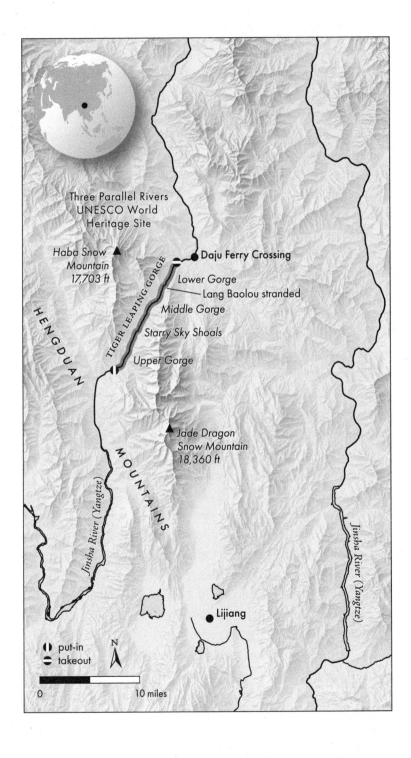

Three Parallel Rivers
UNESCO World
Heritage Site

Haba Snow ▲
Mountain
17,703 ft

HENGDUAN

TIGER LEAPING GORGE

● Daju Ferry Crossing

Lower Gorge
Lang Baolou stranded
Middle Gorge

Starry Sky Shoals

Upper Gorge

Jade Dragon ▲
Snow Mountain
18,360 ft

MOUNTAINS

Jinsha River (Yangtze)

Jinsha River (Yangtze)

● Lijiang

◖ put-in
● takeout

N

0   10 miles

steep gorge walls on the right until the exit from the gorge, twelve miles downstream, where the local crew of the Daju Ferry Crossing formed a final, critical interception line.

Walking down to the observation and main interception site, team leader Maojun Wang saw, far upstream and barely distinguishable in the huge, white flood, a tiny black dot — the capsule containing Lei Jiansheng and Li Qinjian racing downstream at the mercy of the Yangtze. He broke into a run, arrived panting at riverside, searching upstream for sight of the vessel.

Then nothing, for twenty minutes.

Finally, a radio call. The capsule was stuck, recirculating endlessly in the first large eddy. After another long thirty minutes, Wang sought a high vantage point and focused his binoculars upstream. Lang Baoluo, a stalwart of the team from the very beginning, waded deep into the surging river, trying to push the bulky vessel through the eddy line into the main current. A thin rope tethered around his waist traced back to a member of the Sichuan Team on belay from the wet rocky shore. Wang estimated that they were perhaps six hundred feet from the maw of the Upper Tiger Leaping Gorge itself — certain death for a swimmer.

With a final heave by Lang Baoluo, the capsule broke free of its imprisonment. It flushed downstream, turned turtle in a steep hole, and disappeared under tons of recirculating water. Within, the flashlight failed, and in total darkness the battered occupants struggled to breathe as the sides of the capsule crushed inward and jets of water shot through a torn hatch. The capsule suddenly bounded into the air, its terrified passengers momentarily hanging weightless, before plunging again into the torrent, rebounded off cushions of water piling against the gigantic boulders, and finally washed into a huge eddy on the left.

Lei Jiansheng and Li Qinjian emerged from their black rubber cave to cheers from the gathered observers and volleys of gunfire into the air by exuberant reeducation officers. "Long live the great Chinese people," they shouted in unison to the voracious cameras. As the assembled press mobbed the pair, arguing about the exact time of the victory, declaring that a thousand-year legend had been broken that day, Maojun Wang's elation and sense of vindication were tempered. The Middle and Lower Tiger Leaping gorges lay downstream.

1450 hours, September 12, 1986

A few more days to recoup, to make repairs to the capsule, and to scout for intercept sites along the sheer walls that flanked both sides of the middle gorge would have been useful, but the Sichuan Team pressed close behind. The day before Captain Wang Yan and Li Dafang had successfully run the Upper Gorge in their own sealed vessel, named the *Chinese Warrior*.

A split seam in the Luoyang capsule was hastily patched from the inside with a red air mattress. Lang Baoluo, the reader and intellectual who had originally proposed the expedition and who had jumped into the river to wrestle Lei Jiansheng and Li Qinjian back into the flow during their triumph, slid into the capsule. Sun Zhiling, a thirty-five-year-old railway worker nicknamed Toad and universally liked for his ready talk and humor, was the other occupant. With renewed confidence from their triumph above, the Luoyang Team launched downstream again.

Even before the walls closed in to form the Middle Gorge itself, the capsule capsized repeatedly in a huge train of exploding waves at a section called Starry Sky. The capsule was ripped apart and swept into the gorge, where its occupants could be seen clinging for life to the remaining hull. The raft with two swimmers disappeared beneath the next churning ledge, and when it resurfaced thirty seconds later, the horrified observers on the left wall could see but one.

Walking up from the catch site between the middle and lower gorges to see what was causing the delay, Maojun Wang's worst fears became reality. No, an old villager told him, he had not seen the overdue capsule. But he had seen a mysterious, bright red object racing

down the river. Wang's heart thudded in his chest. That could only
be the air mattress patch — and it could only be floating free if the
capsule had been ripped apart.

1800 hours, September 12, 1986
As dusk and night chill gathered, Baoluo crouched, minuscule within
a jumble of angular slabs of fallen rock on the right side of the river,
where a section of cliff had broken off to form a small cleft in the
sheer face and an eddy, which had miraculously caught him and the
remnants of the capsule. Above, in sublime grandeur, towered thousands of feet of canyon wall: lush green vegetation slashed by raw scars
of rockfalls near the river; surmounted by barren faces of contorted,
steely limestones foxed with pink granitic inclusions; and, seemingly
detached from the earth entirely, the gleaming icy summits of the Jade
Dragon Snow Mountains.

His Luoyang teammates and would-be rescuers grouped on the
opposite shore, barely three hundred feet away yet helpless to cross,
or even to shout across, the thundering flow. With desperate arm
signals, they indicated that Baoluo must not attempt to climb, that
he must remain where he was, without food, severely battered, and
stripped naked but for a sodden T-shirt and yellow life jacket. The
only possibility for rescue was for them to find their way above him
on the far shore and drop him a rope from a ledge 120 feet above his
position. They built and maintained a bonfire so that Baoluo could see
and know through the cold and hungry night that his comrades were
there. Of Sun Zhiling there had been no trace.

Search-and-rescue was the priority of all in the following days.
Director Hou ceased preparations of the Sichuan Scientific Team and
threw his members into the effort. Local government officials offered
all support. The media clustered opposite the stranded Baoluo and
argued whether his making it alive to that point constituted a "successful" run of the Middle Tiger Leaping Gorge. An ethnic Naxi villager

was found who frequently gathered herbs across the river. Yes, he assured them, he had been to the critical ledge and could guide them there. They would need to cross the river at the ferry below the lower gorge, then work their way on foot back upstream.

1700 hours, September 13, 1986

The rescue team appeared on the right gorge wall, directly above Baoluo, but from their vantage they could not see him down the steep and unstable chute of broken rock, nor could he hear their shouts above the river. Lacking radios, the rescue operation resorted to a crude three-way pantomime of arm signals back and forth from Wang on the left wall, who could be seen by both. An initial attempt to drop a bundle of food and clothing was foiled by powerful canyon winds. A doubled rope did make it to Baoluo, who secured it around his waist. It tangled and wedged in the shattered rock, however, when they tried to pull him up, and the section nearest Baoluo soon frayed so badly that he had to signal a halt. He was doomed to yet another night without food or clothing, although his rescuers were just yards away. There was still no trace of Sun Zhiling.

1500 hours, September 16, 1986

It had taken two more days to assemble and position, but a rope ladder with bamboo rungs, food, and clothing finally reached Baoluo. Alternately climbing, resting, and being pulled with a belay rope, it took the emaciated and hypothermic victim two hours to ascend the 120 feet. The cheering from the far shore — media, soldiers, prisoners, and the two rival rafting teams — was even more ecstatic than after the upper gorge success. For Baoluo's teammates, however, their elation was tempered by the presumed drowning of Sun Zhiling.

To the rival Chinese teams now literally in the middle of the Tiger Leaping Gorge, astonishing word arrived from five hundred miles upstream. Their dreaded nemesis, the world-famous, lavishly equipped Sino-USA expedition, had quit the river, abandoned the field. Details were sketchy, but the game had changed.

Ken Warren and the Sino-USA Expedition had launched down the river on July 21, first in inflatable kayaks on the shallow upper reaches, then in seven 18-foot oar-rigged whitewater rafts laden with tons of equipment: propane stoves with tanks of fuel, gasoline generators, thirty-seven waterproof cases of camera gear, food, and camp gear for the crew of fifteen. Progress was slow, and they began to fall steadily behind the optimistic timeline drawn up in advance by Ken Warren and the China Sports Service. Rations fell short on the long legs between road-accessible resupply points.

Three days after the rafts drifted downstream from their base camp at Tuotuoheyan, with 540 miles to cover before the next road, David Shippee, a twenty-eight-year-old aspiring photographer from Idaho, fell gravely ill from altitude sickness, and the following day, July 31, at 11:24 P.M., expedition doctor David Gray pronounced his death. With no way to preserve or evacuate his remains, they buried him with a simple ceremony beside the river. In this upper stretch the Chinese name is the Tongtian Ho, the "River to Heaven."[*]

Shaken and demoralized, the Sino-USA Expedition proceeded downstream for eleven more days, friction growing over perceived inequities in the division of camp chores and dwindling food supplies, and resentment of Ken Warren's autocratic leadership. Team cohesion continued to unravel upon their rendezvous with Jan Warren and the road support team. Heightening the tension, they learned that roughly

---

[*] Shippee had suffered distress since the expedition's arrival at altitude, but he declared that he was recovered and insisted on accompanying the rafts down the long, isolated leg of the river. He, like Yao Maoshu the previous year, in the end risked all for the dream of a career as a professional photographer. If Chinese news reporter Wang Ming, who died in a rockfall covering the Chinese attempts in Tiger Leaping Gorge for *Youth World* magazine, is included, the toll of recording the Yangtze attempts was three — by drowning, pulmonary edema, and rockfall.

three weeks before, several Chinese rafters had been killed somewhere just downstream.* To date, the expedition had faced bitter cold, sickness, hunger, and the delays of navigating the shallow, braided stream. Now they were about to face massive whitewater, and the lack of any detail about the Chinese tragedy only heightened fears of the unknown. Four of the Americans had had enough. Expedition doctor David Gray, and oarsmen Bill Atwood, Gary Peebles, and Toby Sprinkle, departed base camp on August 15 to make their way home.

A consolidated expedition launched downstream two days later: four rafts joined by experienced kayaker Paul Sharpe, on a river now swollen to 12,500 cubic feet per second. Things went well initially, and at the next road crossing they were joined by still photographer Kevin O'Brien and Chinese magazine reporter Chen Qun. Soon thereafter they encountered their first big rapid, a huge roostertail wave exploding into the eastern cliff wall, and the game changed.

Ironically, Warren's Sino-USA Expedition and the rival Chinese teams now found themselves in similar situations: needing to run every rapid and having to invent unconventional means of doing so when the size of the rapids exceeded the limits of their conventional rafts and the skills of their oarsmen. The Americans had no tradition that suggested portaging rapids that were too dangerous amounted to a dishonorable failure, as the Chinese had decided, but Warren believed that the answer to punching through big rapids lay in sheer mass and momentum. He had chosen rafts with solid floors that filled with tons of water until bailed, and lavish camera and camp equipment he considered a bonus.

At this first big rapid, however, they initially attempted to portage, and the carry of just one raft, its oars and boxes of gear, took the entire team four backbreaking hours — time they could ill afford and for

---

*In a rare, and disastrous, attempt at cooperation, an early prototype of the Chinese enclosed capsules was trapped and pummeled for half an hour in an enormous hole. As their horrified teammates watched, it was finally torn apart by the relentless beating and ejected the lifeless bodies of Kong Zhiyi of the Sichuan Team and Zhang Jun and Yang Honglin of the Luoyang Team.

which they had not planned. Abandoning the portage, they elected to try a method more to Warren's liking, one that had been experimented with years earlier on the Colorado but had never found acceptance. Over the next two hours, they lashed together the three remaining rafts, deliberately filled them halfway with water for extra weight, and, shortly before dark, maneuvered the awkward craft into the current. It wallowed down the long tongue, accelerating into the giant pulsing roostertail, which exploded, slamming all three conjoined rafts into the cliff wall, bending frames, breaking oars, puncturing one raft and a propane tank. It was the following day before the separated elements of the expedition — the portaged raft and crew, the crippled three-raft experiment, and camera crews scattered along the cliffs — were reunited.

That had been, Warren declared to the TV camera, the biggest whitewater he had ever seen. He doubled down, lashing all four rafts together.

The mammoth contraption, its four rafts awash with river water, proved to have little more maneuverability than the Chinese fully enclosed capsules. They washed downstream for two miles after the first rapid before they could halt in an eddy, and later, when the kayak scout ahead walkie-talkied back that there was a blind drop ahead, it was already too late. For ninety screaming minutes, the rig hurtled downstream over ledges, into holes, and around bends, spewing passengers and gear, breaking steel frames, gashing float chambers, dragging its hapless crew into the unknown.

They fared no better the next day. Again Paul Sharpe kayaked ahead, found monstrous rapids, called for the raft rig to stop. Again they were unable to heed his direction, and again they were sucked inexorably into unscouted whitewater. Sharp rocks frayed the ropes lashing the rafts together. Gigantic waves folded the rig like a huge piece of rubberized nylon origami, catapulting Warren and several of the crew into the river. Again they washed helplessly downstream for more than an hour. It was a somber bivouac that evening when they finally fetched up in an eddy by shore, knowing that they had survived not by planning, nor skill, but only by the river's mercy. They were in deep trouble, and one by one they realized just how much.

After a tentative foray downstream in his kayak, Paul Sharpe crossed the river and struck out on foot on river left to find Jan Warren at the next base camp and initiate an overland rescue. Ken Warren himself went next, hiking down on river right to see what lay ahead, then, instead of returning to report his findings, striking out directly for the base camp. Leaderless, running out of food, and with several men ill with dysentery, the remaining rafters and film crew finally abandoned the river too. Reality had overcome the dream.

Morning, September 21, 1986

After the shocking events of the past few days, the dramatic rescue of Baoluo and the devastating loss of Sun Zhiling,* team leader Maojun Wang was determined to attempt the Lower Tiger Leaping Gorge himself. The dank reserve capsule smelled of vomit and stale sweat as he and high school physical education teacher Li Weimin slid into their places and made their final checks: lights on, knife secured, oxygen ready, openings lashed closed.

Wang played through in his mind what they had scouted downstream. Constricting mountains forced the river rolling down from the middle gorge into a sharp zigzag, smashing alternately into the left and right cliff faces in gigantic exploding pillows. At the crux point, named Daojiao Beach, the river dropped 115 vertical feet over the course of a mile and a half. It appeared much more dangerous than the Upper Tiger Leaping section and was perhaps exceeded only by the Starry Sky Shoals. He gave the release command.

A deafening cannonade of sound engulfed the capsule, and Wang's warning shout that they were entering Daojiao Beach was cut short

---

* They would recover his body two weeks later, far downstream.

mid-sentence. Their vessel began to flip repeatedly. Around them the
capsule wrenched and contorted as it was alternately crushed underwater and rebounded into the air. Water flooded the compartment,
forcing its way into their mouths and noses. After five full loops, the
motion settled into a rapid spinning and periodic bumps; they fought
back waves of nausea and growing anxiety as they recirculated in a
gigantic eddy. Local Naxi villagers spoke of logs trapped for a month
or more in such places, but after forty-five minutes a fluke wave tossed
the capsule back into the downstream torrent.

When he felt their movement slow, Wang cautiously unlashed the
capsule entrance. Blinking in the unaccustomed sunlight, he gulped
the fresh air, and the first thing he saw was the crimson Chinese flag
of their recovery team. At 1:05 P.M., September 21, 1986, Tiger Leaping
Gorge lay behind them.

September 24, 1986
Not to be outdone, and striving for a cleaner run of the entire Tiger
Leaping Gorge, the Sichuan Team's brick-red *Chinese Warrior* capsule,
manned by their experienced raft captain, Wang Yan, accompanied by
Yan Ke, launched above the middle gorge. In a single wild ride, the
pair flushed through the Starry Sky Shoals and the Middle Canyon.
Failing to wash into any eddies, they shot the length of the Lower
Canyon as well. At 1:33 P.M. Wang Yan emerged from the hatch, flashing his characteristic delighted smile and squinting as water poured
from his mop of black hair, the first person to survive the full length of
the Tiger Leaping Gorge.

Each in his own way, Maojun Wang and Wang Yan had made
Chinese, and whitewater, history.

With the symbolic crux of the river challenge behind them, and the
Sino-USA Expedition off the table, the rival Chinese teams raced

to complete their mutual source-to-sea goal. Elements went back upstream to complete segments both had leapfrogged by vehicle in their race to Tiger Leaping Gorge. Others continued downstream toward the head of commercial navigation. Neither mission was easy; five more died by drowning. By the time the two teams reached the East China Sea in November, the race down the Yangtze had cost the lives of one rafter in 1985, and, in 1986, nine Chinese rafters, one American rafter and photographer, and a Chinese journalist killed by a rock-fall in Tiger Leaping Gorge. Looking back in 2016 from thirty years' perspective, Yang Yong from the Sichuan Scientific Team reflected, "I joined the expedition team not simply out of patriotism. I was motivated by a curiosity about the Yangtze that started in my childhood, so when there was this chance to raft down this mystic river, I joined. Yet with the competitive atmosphere getting stronger, the nature of the descents deviated from what I had originally intended. Looking back, I'd say it was a tragic ending with so many young people losing their lives."

CHAPTER NINE

The Hardest Thing, in
the Purest Style

The Stikine River

I now define a line as a route that takes you through a
rapid — and into the rest of your life.
— Doug Ammons

At the end of summer in 1992, Doug Ammons loaded his boat, revealed his destination to no one, and drove seventeen hundred miles north from Missoula, Montana, into the heart of the Canadian wilderness. Driving day and night through a cold mist and rain that heralded autumn in the North, resisting the mesmerizing sweep of the windshield wipers, he knew that his objective, the Grand Canyon of the Stikine River in northwestern British Columbia, was whitewater at the very limits of kayakers' skills and equipment. The extra hazards of mostly unclimbable canyon walls and surrounding wilderness made it one of the most demanding runs anywhere in the world. No one had ever attempted that canyon alone.

Beginning in the 1970s and throughout the 1980s, kayakers in the northwestern United States had aggressively pushed the limits of their skills and ever-more-durable plastic boats, in steep, high-volume whitewater. The North Fork of the Payette River in Idaho in particular became a training ground, with challenging powerful rapids paralleled by a road that facilitated access and rescue. With increasing confidence and skill, they also began looking north, to the rugged cordillera of the Rocky Mountains in Canada and Alaska, to push the limits of expedition whitewater.

In 1971 pioneering Idaho kayaker Walt Blackadar stunned the whitewater world with a solo, two-day run of Turnback Canyon on the Alsek River in British Columbia. The following year, with Kay Swanson and Roger Hazelwood, he ran the Devils Canyon of the Susitna River in Alaska. Blackadar returned to the Susitna in 1977 with Rob Lesser of Boise, Idaho, who, along with Don Banducci, the following year became the first to run the North Fork of the Payette continuously from top to bottom and who would go on to take expedition kayaking to whole new levels in the 1980s.

Lesser had heard rumor of a canyon on the Stikine River in British Columbia, and, driving north to meet Blackadar on the Susitna, he chartered a plane in Dease Lake to overfly it. What he saw was stunning, beyond anything he had ever considered running. For forty-five miles, ten to twenty thousand cubic feet of water per second cascaded down as much as 120 feet per mile, compressed into violent turbulence, huge holes, and monstrous lateral slabs of flow by thousand-foot walls so narrow he could not see many sections of the river under their overhang where, even on the river, paddlers would be at risk from falling rock. Grizzlies and wolves patrolled the surrounding highlands; mountain goats stood sentinel on its cliffs. Just upstream, under a rickety steel-grated bridge that carried the Cassiar Highway over the river, the Stikine flowed and waited for its Mallory and Irvine, its Hillary and Tenzing Norgay, its Messner.

Rob Lesser had taken up the challenge of the Stikine in 1981, with strong western kayakers Lars Holbeck, John Wasson, Don Banducci, and Rick Fernald. Like Richard Bangs on the Zambezi, they enlisted the financial and helicopter support of ABC's *American Sportsman*, with producer John Wilcox and field director Roger Brown. The rapids were even bigger than Lesser had appreciated from the aerial scout. In one huge recirculating hole, since named Wasson's Hole, John Wasson very nearly drowned. In his own words: "I got sucked into the hole; the lights went out. I was ripped out of my boat and rag-dolled deep underwater in God's gyroscope. I had a long time to think what that first breath of water was going to feel like." He did wash out, barely conscious, to be rescued by his teammates.

That first attempt had to be abandoned about two-thirds of the way through the canyon due to time and helicopter constraints, but the *American Sportsman* film was spectacular. Upon seeing it, twenty-four-year-old classical guitarist, swimmer, and martial artist Doug Ammons thought kayaking might be the sport for him. In any sport, midtwenties might be considered late to begin if one's goal is to reach elite levels, but Doug himself felt that he had been preparing for this his entire life, albeit in unconventional ways.

Doug had grown up in a tumultuous family of seven siblings in the university town of Missoula, a crucible combining the intellectual rigor and student unrest of the University of Montana in the late 1960s and early 1970s, where both his parents were PhDs and researchers; the demanding sports leagues of the American West; and especially the nearby Bitterroot wilderness of the Rocky Mountains, his refuge at an early age. There he camped and hiked and climbed and canoed, sometimes with his younger brother and friends, equally content to be alone in the vast surroundings.

Doug emerged an amalgam of rebellious iconoclast and introverted overachiever: If anyone said something was impossible, that was his starting point. He practiced judo, absorbing the philosophy of the martial arts as well as the physical skills, quickly moving up through the belts. From age eight on he was a nationally ranked youth league swimmer. Yet he declined athletic scholarships at prestigious universities because he was unwilling to submit to a coach's demands for his exclusive time and attention.

Sophisticated high school science projects won Doug statewide awards and accolades from university researchers, and despite all his other interests he progressed steadily toward a PhD on perceptual learning. Yet he was determined to avoid the clannish hegemony within academia, which he had observed firsthand through his mother and father.

At age seventeen Doug discovered classical guitar. To his natural athleticism and the disciplines of competitive swimming and judo, this brought a new aesthetic element and required melding flawless technique and effortless flow, to where everything technical disappears and only the flow remains. It fed his lust to excel, and he did. Within three years, often practicing eight or more hours per day, he was studying with one of the best concert guitarists in the world, Christopher Parkening. Yet he disliked sharing his music with concert audiences; the music was a conversation for himself alone, and he was unsure where the guitar could take him.

Then, inspired by the TV film of Rob Lesser on the Stikine, he discovered the rivers, with their universal rhythms, their perfect flow, and he took up kayaking in earnest. In vivid dreams, in color and sound, he flowed with the water. On clear sun-dappled streams, he seemed to levitate above the river bottom. He would surf across swelling waves, every stroke and lean part of a perfect melodic line. Then, in a suspended dissonance and grand finale, he would plunge his bow deep into the trough of downstream-flowing water, launching the kayak and himself briefly into the sky end over end to view the clear flow below.

As he progressed, Doug found in the icy chaos of big rapids a mighty fugue of athletic challenge and that elemental danger that transforms the merely beautiful into the sublime. Here was an inhuman power that demanded nothing of him yet offered the impossible. His kayak became for him a magnificent instrument that allowed him to play the music of the flowing planet, with every mood possible from gentle meander to irresistible, crushing power. A discipline worthy of his devotion.

Doug threw himself into his new passion with the same insomniac intensity he applied to myriad other facets of his life: his young family, his PhD dissertation, his music. He trained compulsively on the freezing winter river in Missoula. He fell in with Rob Lesser, Bob McDougall, and other leading paddlers, who welcomed him into their small fraternity, and before the end of his second season he was training on the North Fork of the Payette and other classic runs in the Northwest. He welcomed the new doors other paddlers were throwing open and the extraordinary comradery engendered by shared challenges and risks. It was their moment on a cutting edge in their sport. They eagerly researched new runs, experimented with new paddling techniques, and forged deep bonds.

Yet beyond the North American Rockies, Doug saw a wider world as well. He read of the shocking failure of Ken Warren's attempt on the Yangtze in *Outside* magazine, and, in the university library that had been his second home since childhood, he read in Chinese magazines of the bizarre success of the Chinese teams in the biggest whitewater ever attempted. And transcending geography, there was a special, almost mystical, connection Doug felt to the moving water itself, an element beyond the joys of athleticism and teamwork that he was unable to share.

Rob Lesser returned to the Stikine with Lars Holbeck and Bob McDougall in 1985 and achieved a first descent through the complete canyon, running most of the rapids, again with a film crew and helicopter support. The canyon was starting to come into focus. They assigned names to the major rapids; they knew a bit about the lines and hazards — at least at specific water levels. Then, in 1989, Rob invited Doug to join him and McDougall for a first attempt Alpine-style, completely self-supported, without the helicopter. The logical next stage: a purer style.

The expedition became a disaster at the very first big rapid. As Doug watched, helpless and terrified, his close friend McD almost died, trashed in a hole, ejected from his boat, then pinned underwater in a boulder sieve. He miraculously clawed his way back to air and shore, but, unable to move either upstream or down, he again came near death free-soloing a four-hundred-foot vertical face of crumbling rock to escape the canyon.

They aborted that run, but the following year Lesser and Doug were joined by Tom Schibig for another Alpine-style attempt, the three paddling strongly as a team. They did not run every drop, but they shared the adrenaline-pumped scouting, the mutual support in decision making, the reassurance of rescue plans, the collective tasks in rock-climbing portages and nighttime bivouacs, and the elation and relief of each success. In an exhilarating three days, the team achieved Rob Lesser's decade-long goal. For Doug, that indescribable presence he felt on all moving water, that bass note just below audible, the color just beyond ultraviolet, the movement at the edge of peripheral vision had been more profound and powerful than he had ever experienced. But it had been curtained behind the urgent demands of teamwork with Rob and Tom.

Two years after that team success, it was near dusk as Doug pulled his car off the pitted clay-and-gravel road and donned blue rain pants, faded red anorak, and black watch cap. A cold drizzle condensed in the forest understory, gathering into huge drops that spattered to the ground, and during gaps in the mist he could see the snowline perhaps four hundred feet above. Three days' dark stubble on the angular planes of his face testified to his seventeen-hundred-mile drive north from Missoula. Arms akimbo, his feet shoulder-width apart, like a silent martial artist ready to face his ultimate test, he gazed intently at the huge gray river that had consumed his dreams for a decade. This time, without the filter of inter-human dynamics, he was going to find what it was about the canyon, and about himself, that he had only glimpsed so faintly before. *The hardest thing, in the purest style. There were many places of truth in the grandeur of the natural world,* Doug believed, *but for him there was no greater arena on this planet than the Grand Canyon of the Stikine River.**

---

* Thoughts and images in *italics* are from Doug Ammons's unpublished memoir.

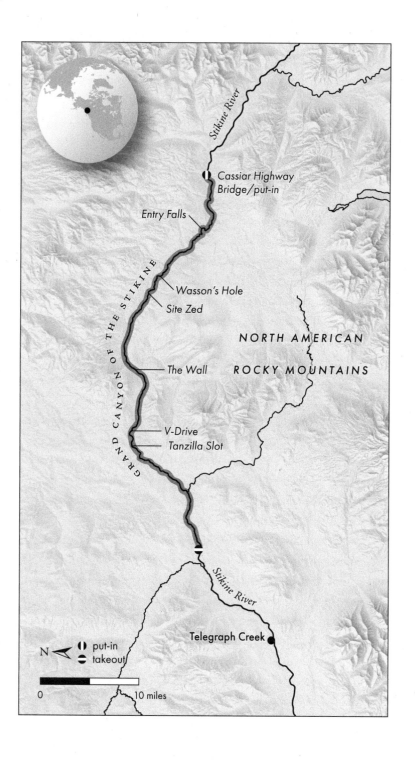

Stikine River

Cassiar Highway
Bridge/put-in

Entry Falls

GRAND CANYON OF THE STIKINE

Wasson's Hole

Site Zed

NORTH AMERICAN

ROCKY MOUNTAINS

The Wall

V-Drive

Tanzilla Slot

Stikine River

Telegraph Creek

N

put-in
takeout

0   10 miles

No longer occupied by driving, by the rain and the mud, his mind raced wildly to what he was about to encounter. In a routine he had practiced on dozens of previous kayak expeditions and had rehearsed in his mind for months while planning this one, Doug checked and rechecked each precious item of his ultralight gear, testing where everything would fit inside his boat to maintain perfect balance. After a few minutes, however, the rote activity could no longer distract him from images that crowded in from the dripping forest and leaped unbidden into his mind.

He pictured himself standing on the soaking cliffs miles downstream, somewhere near the Narrows, getting ready for what was coming, carefully weighing each footstep and handhold, feeling the threat of the river grow. There's an oddly familiar sound, and he turns around. His little daughter is there, huddling in the rocks behind him, afraid and cold in the wind. Her hair is dirty and wet. She's crying.

He startled, and knives of adrenaline shot through him. The physical and chemical response was irrational, but some part of him did it without thought. He shook his head to push the image away, to concentrate on the present danger of the river.

The child's image came again, floating before his eyes, and the anxiety returned in little jabs down his arms. His worlds collided. *How would he take care of her? She's so small and weak. And the other little ones? They tire so quickly. The gray, roiling water below is so threatening. It will snatch them away from him before he can react, and he'll be left with emptiness.*

Again, he shook the image away. The feeling of vulnerability brings fear. *Alone, he is strong.*

He walked back to the car, fished a scrap of paper and pen out of the glove box to write a note to leave for his wife, Robin — just in case. He sat immobile, pen poised, but could not think clearly, and no words would come. He felt as though he was cracking open a door that had to be kept closed. Beyond lay the possibility that he might die, that he could not do what he had set out before himself. Images flickered from beyond that forbidden crack.

Rocks falling from a cliff above, he can hear their click and whistle.
Reflexively, he shoved his hand out to ward the feeling away, but another image came instead.

He feels the river burying him, cold pressure all around, and he's spinning downward into darkness.

"No," he shouted in rage into the dripping forest. "This is bullshit!" He crumpled the unmarked paper into a ball and threw it into the footwell. To open that door would lead to quitting, or to the fear that would bring certain death. They would find the car and know. When did not matter, and he was unable to write why.

Unbidden, past and future swarmed around Doug the following morning as he clambered along the steep shoreline to scout the first big drop, Entry Falls. Companions from previous runs hovered just behind him, whispering advice, or appeared in fragmentary glimpses.

The tip of McDougall's blue kayak flashes by in the big hole below a narrow slot on the right. He's trapped! He's cartwheeled, Maytagged, then sucked out of sight under an undercut on one side. He comes up twisting and sculling, sucking at air, then cartwheeling out of control again, fighting for his life while the river strangles him with ice-cold water. The water surges and wedges him beneath the undercut rock. A hand gropes up, searching for purchase, to push out underneath. Slowly the boat reappears, then his head, and then wham, he's back in. The empty blue kayak flushes out of the hole and into the main rapid.

Struggling to focus, Doug tore himself away from his three-year-old nightmare and back to the present. The water was lower now, and with relief he could see that the line where McDougall had almost died was no longer a death trap. Angry with himself for his inability to separate reality from the storm of images and feelings from the past, Doug hurried back to his boat and peeled out toward the line on the right before he could second-guess himself further. He felt shaky, his first few strokes unsure. A series of huge exploding waves bashed him around at the bottom of the drop before he could eddy out far below. Across the river rose cliff, dead vertical, all fissured and shattered rock.

*A tiny figure, three hundred feet up, is McDougall, barefoot and
unroped. A rock flies off the face, arcs, bounces, falls for second after long
second, then slams into the roaring water. An arm reaching, searching for
a hold, a foot moves, he inches up. If he peels off now, he'll bounce like that
rock did then hit the water. Where will his body be when it comes around
this corner? How should I try to get it to shore in this rapid? Will he be
alive? Climb, McD, you son of a bitch! Don't peel off right in front of me.
I'm going to watch you die!*

Those times were over; this was now. But the ghosts followed,
joined by fears of what lay ahead. What the lower water volume and
two years of rock-shattering winter frost and raging summer floods
might mean downstream remained unknowable. Would some rapids
be more constricted, with fewer options? Would the possibilities to
scout and portage have been reconfigured as well? Would there be a
place where he could neither paddle nor portage?

He splashed water on his face. *You wanted to test yourself. You
wanted to see when the seams would begin to show. They are showing now.
How strong are you?*

Even the dozens of unnamed rapids required all his skill and
focus. Giant haystack waves exploded beneath his hull, throwing him
violently ten or more feet to one side or the other. Eddies undulated
and boiled in competition with the downstream current; unpredictable
surges sucked at his stern and catapulted him end over end backward.
The constant action stripped away the shakiness. He was paddling
well now, perhaps the best in his life, muscle memory reacting.

Deliberately, he forced himself to examine his surroundings, to
stay in the moment. The sun appeared briefly, and the canyon walls
burst into color: brilliant yellow poplars hanging precariously from
rain-gleaming rock walls of reds and browns and sooty black. With a
gunshot crack, a rock the size of a basketball exploded against a shelf
fifty yards downstream, and Doug ducked as rock shrapnel ricocheted
off the canyon wall. This was a place of awesome beauty, but no place
to hang around.

A few miles downstream, the thousand-foot canyon walls closed in, and the river vanished over a horizon line in the narrowed slot. Thundering below, Doug knew, lay Wasson's Hole. Here the reality that lay beneath his speculation and fear would be revealed, and now he would have to deal with it.

What about the big scissor-like diagonals right above the hole; will they now be one river-wide hole?

What if there is no line? What are you going to do then? Climb? No one knows you're here. No helicopter from Dease Lake is going to pluck you out.

The answers lay at the only possible overlook, fifty feet above, at the top of a ramp of river-smoothed bedrock on the right shore. He pulled into the surging eddy at its base, clipped a sling of nylon webbing to a wire ring in the boat, slipped his legs out of the cockpit, and stepped precariously onto the wet rock. Straining for a purchase with each step, he heaved the boat up into a slot, snapped a carabiner into the stern grab loop, and roped it securely to a chockstone. A careless slip down into the river, by his boat or himself, would be the end of everything.

From the top of the ramp, fifty feet above the river, Doug balanced precariously on rubble from the cliff face and stared down into his fate. His phantom companions were no longer with him, whispering their warnings and advice. Only a still, small voice in his head and the thudding of his heart.

There is no line!

He fought off panic and tried to analyze the massive drop spread out beneath him. At the lip, a boxcar-sized boulder created a deep, nearly river-wide hole, forcing about a third of the river to the right. Two years before, at higher flow, this had been a steep, plunging ramp of water, their route to skirt past John Wasson's terrifying "God's gyroscope," which consumed the entire left side of the river. But now most of that water plummeted vertically onto broken rock, exploding off in all directions. Down that route would be certain entrapment in the boulder sieve, under tons of crushing water.

The other side of the boulder at the top looked even worse. Most of the river thundered into sheer rock face on the left and plunged downstream. In the center, thirty yards beyond the lip, two massive, exploding diagonal waves fed from right to left, directly into the hole itself.

There is no line!

In desperation he stared up at the thousand-foot cliffs on either side. As he knew already, there was no answer in that direction. He stood, frozen, mind empty. Rain dripped off his helmet visor, and mud trickled off the wall above onto his shoulders. The roar from below filled the canyon. Filled him.

Reluctantly, Doug knew what he had to do: come in off the wall on the left, watch the boils and keep speed while angling to the right down the plunging slide, then punch through the breaking diagonals that flushed into Wasson's Hole. There would be no time to correct a mistake. With even the slightest angle to the left he would be shot deep into the hole. His mind, normally so precise and analytical, refused to calculate the odds that he could pull this off. The odds did not matter — this was what he had to do.

Even if you do everything right, you're still going into Wasson's. Get ready for the beating of your life.

He took one last look to fix the image in his mind, downclimbed carefully to his boat, and slid into the water. The ritual of checking his sprayskirt, helmet strap, and life jacket, felt futile. He splashed cold water on his face. The current sucked him toward the horizon line, toward the end of the world . . .

The first big wave, at the brink, loomed far over his head, bigger even than he had imagined. From its exploding crest, he glimpsed the entirety of the massive drop before him, then felt the momentary weightlessness as he hurtled downward. There was no more time for analysis, fear, or conscious reaction. His brain screamed right — Right, RIGHT — as instinct took over. Two strokes in the water ripping down the ramp. Flattening himself forward, small against the deck, he slammed into the first big diagonal, engulfed in an explosion of gray water jamming him left, every muscle straining, desperately feathering with his paddle to maintain his angle to the right as he was consumed by the second diagonal.

After seemingly endless churning, the maelstrom released its grip, and, shaking the water from his eyes as he emerged from the wall of froth and chaos, he found himself in mid-river, staring down into the grinding maw of Wasson's Hole directly ahead. Several desperate strokes right — Right, RIGHT — and a miracle of exploding water threw him past. The terror flashed by on his left, then receded behind him. Thrown about in the turbulence of the runout, just sixteen seconds after he had crested the first wave and seen the rapid spread out below him, he turned back toward the drop, teeth bared like a frenzied wild animal. No sound came from his lips, but his insides were screaming *I'm through!*

He slumped forward onto the deck of his kayak and made no attempt to check the tears that streamed down his face.

Doug built no fire his first night within the canyon but let the solitude press in. The sobbing children had remained at the put-in, along with the note he could not write to Robin. The phantom companions from previous runs, who had crowded around him at the first big rapids, helping him scout, discussing the lines, whispering warnings and advice, had fallen away as the afternoon passed. There was now no past and no future, no other human presence, and into that void the river was reaching out to him, into him.

On impulse, as the long northern twilight turned to darkness, he stripped off his clothes and stepped naked into a shallow cleft in the shoreline rock where the Stikine surged in and out. He welcomed the embrace of the frigid water, felt the caress of thousands of tiny bubbles from the aerated flow, and pressed his palms against the rock to resist the siren tide as each pulse of the river urged his body out into the downstream current.

Above, eons of bedrock cliffs, the detritus of warm Paleozoic seas, intertwined with basalts and pyroclastics from the maw of the Pacific

Ring of Fire, shot upward to disappear into low-hanging mist. Below where he lay, below where the river gnawed its inevitable path, he could sense the black rock plunging downward too, down through the slow tectonic chaos into the tortured mantle of the Earth. Somewhere beyond intellect and words, he was touching the very powers that create the planet.

Cold forced him from his inchoate ecstasy, back to his sleeping bag, and he woke early to a clearing sky, pink and purple altocumulus. Bright sunlight crept down the upper canyon wall across the river, setting the yellow aspen ablaze, even as his camp would remain in deep shadow for hours yet. A single goat, brilliant white on the dark, lichen-streaked rock, stared down, secure and at ease in its savage home. Doug built a small fire and enjoyed the luxuries of hot oatmeal and pulling on an unfrozen wet suit.

His day began with the simple, brutal labor of his first portage. This was Site Zed, a huge, long rapid that none of the previous expeditions had run, and he had already determined to pass it by as well. With his gear-laden boat hung awkwardly on one shoulder, for almost an hour he clambered alternately through house-sized boulder labyrinths, where floodwaters had scoured out any rock smaller than twelve or fifteen feet in diameter, and across wildly unstable talus slopes at the base of the cliff. Avoiding falls required the utmost concentration, a distraction and relief after the fears, visions, and agonizing choices of the previous day. He was surprised to find that even in the dark shadow he was sweating copiously in his neoprene. His breath came in quick pants, and he had to stop frequently for long breaks. At the end of the portage, he gulped handful after handful of river water from a surging eddy, then sat for half an hour and more, arms and legs aching from lactic buildup, mind and body still reeling from the previous day's cascade of dopamine, serotonin, and endorphins.

Eventually he concluded that he must move on, that he would gain nothing by more rest. *What next? You're only a third of the way down.*

To shut the voice off, he slowly ran his finger across the sharp broken edge of a boulder. *This is life. Here. Now. Pay attention.*

Doug scouted, then ran, the last big drop of Site Zed, difficult enough in its own right, and proceeded as cautiously as he could downstream, scouting four or five times in the next several miles. He feared that with the lower water, spots that he had run before along powerful diagonal chutes might now be river-wide holes, with no spot to punch through or under. But in rapid after rapid, he could feel the lines, with a deep certainty that the water would deliver him to his destination — if only he asked the right questions and worked with it to give the right answers.

The steep gradient eased off momentarily, the gray river pulsing regularly up and down, swirling in leisurely whirlpools, its power in check, lurking, gathering strength beneath his hull. In a quiet eddy beside the cliff face, he reached out and pressed hands and face against the smooth dark stone, cold and polished by eons of flowing water and glacial sand. He could feel the immensity of the canyon, its power infinite, yet intimate in the polished rock. With a start, he was jerked from his reverie to see his paddle drifting away downstream, one blade sucked lazily down into the slate-gray water, the other turning slow circles above the surface. In near panic, he hand-paddled over to snatch it up.

Doug recognized a steep talus slope on his right, found a spot to pull out on the left, about eighty yards upstream from the Wall. This was a major drop, one that could not be bypassed on either side of the river. Two years before, they had carried the top half, then run the bottom section more or less blindly. There had been no spot from which they could see it well, even rock climbing. They made it that day, in that water. Today he would again be tested, like at Wasson's Hole.

He traversed along crack systems and small handholds, directly above the water sweeping into the Wall, to a little scoured cave, its floor covered with gravel, twenty feet above the river. He could see the

upper section laid out below him, huge and complex, but not as bad
as it had appeared before, when they carried along the talus slope on
the right to put in halfway down. The bottom half remained a mystery.
He inched back onto the rock face, twenty yards to another vantage
point, a six-inch ledge with a good handhold for his left hand. Gripping tightly and leaning out as far as he could, he could barely glimpse
the heart of the drop.

From this precarious overlook he could not see well enough to
perform his usual detailed analysis, to calculate the odds, to plan and
visualize each paddle stroke. There were certainly killer holes on both
sides going in. The only feasible line led down the chaotic center, and
farther toward the bottom were additional pourovers* and holes —
impossible to judge for size but sure to be gigantic. Unlike the day
before at Wasson's, today his intuition projected confidence, not fear.
If the river could find its way, so could he. Rather, he and the river
together.

He eased his way back across the wet rock face, taking care with each
hand- and foothold, settled firmly into his boat, cautioned himself to
curb his impatience, and ran through his pre-run ritual: running his
hands over sprayskirt, life jacket, helmet strap, paddle. Moments later,
he emerged from a fugue of power strokes, spins on the brief tops
of waves and boils, tight curls forward onto the deck of his kayak as
he was engulfed in crashing foam, diagonal explosions slingshotting
him around and past thunderous holes. He washed through a chaotic
runout of irregular breaking waves at least ten or twelve feet high, not
even trying to control the boat, content to be thrown about at random.

We made it, he shouted in his mind, not sure whether the we
referred to the river or to his kayak.

He bivouacked that night on the left bank, in a grove of aspen on a
big sandbar — the only sandbar on the entire run. Leaning comfort-
ably against a rock, he gazed across his small fire down to the river,

---

* Rocks near the surface but covered by flowing water.

here slick and wide. He could feel the temperature dropping on his exposed back. It would freeze overnight, he knew. Dinner consisted of a can of sardines folded into four pieces of bread, half of a peanut butter and jelly sandwich, and a PowerBar, all washed down with river water.

It had been a remarkably good day; he felt that he had breached some mental barrier with his paddling, had achieved a new level. He had been rigorously training his physical skills for years as well as developing a powerful intuitive sense of the moving water. Now, however, his connection to the river was more intense, his confidence in his own judgment more secure. He had tested the limits of his nerve and judgment in the past two days as never before, pushing closer and closer to that edge where overconfidence would kill. But proving himself also meant recognizing exactly where that edge lay — knowing when and where to back off. He was glad he had chosen to portage around the upper part of Site Zed, and today he had taken extra time and energy to scout ahead on foot at almost every drop.

The trunk of an aspen behind him bore the claw marks of a grizzly, from higher than Doug could reach down to the ground, and crisp tracks in the damp sand were, he estimated, not more than two days old. There were wolf tracks too, in abundance, including the miniature tracks of pups. He studied those intently, envisioning the pups gamboling, springing into the air, tussling with one another. The presence of other living creatures seemed oddly comforting. In his experience, animals in the wilderness usually preferred to keep to themselves, but even if the grizzly were to return, that was, like a rapid far downstream, a situation to be dealt with when it became reality, not a fear to dominate his present.

After breakfast Doug packed up his gear and his remaining food: two PowerBars and half a peanut butter and jelly sandwich. It was going to be a long, hard day. Harder and hungrier if he did not make it all the way out. There were several big, difficult drops that would require careful scouting and all his skill and judgment: Wall II,

Scissors, the Hole That Ate Chicago. But V-drive was in a class by itself — the last big crux point to be faced.

Once again, the rain-and-lichen-streaked walls closed in, reducing the sky to a narrow slit, and the river ahead disappeared, only an urgent pulsing roar revealing its downward course. They had portaged V-drive at river level on the left two years previously, but what changes had two years of erosion and flood wrought? Though not as persistent or as intense as on the first day, the fears nevertheless leaped at him in a mental ambush.

From a pinnacle one hundred feet above the river, V-drive lay spread out before him, roaring and exploding into gleaming mist as the sun pierced straight down into the depths of the canyon. It was as deadly as he remembered. The water dropped twenty feet or more, slamming into the right wall in a diagonal curler a dozen feet high, then ricocheted off a truck-sized boulder in another diagonal. There was not much pillow boiling up against the boulder. Was it undercut? On the left the water plunged directly into a sieve of boulders fallen from the cliffs above. Pinning would be almost certain.

But the portage on the left was still there. He leaned against the rock wall and sobbed with relief.

The portage route led directly across the tops of the boulders forming the lethal sieve on the left, a delicate balancing act with his shouldered boat and gear. On a flat, house-sized boulder in the middle, he allowed himself a break, ate his last half sandwich, and contemplated the tons of water screaming into the cliff wall at eye level across the river. As he stared, mesmerized, he began to see a possible line. He could feel the acceleration as he plunged down the steep ramping tongue, then leaned hard right as his body merged into the diagonal explosion off the right wall, rebounding left . . .

There is a line.

He smiled and shook his head. This one, he would leave.

Maybe next time.

The Tanzilla Slot, the dramatic escape hatch from the Stikine Canyon, was not difficult compared with what lay behind him. But it was very, very weird. Between sun-bright orange and yellow cliffs above on either side, a colossal plug of dark basalt blocked the entire river, cleft only by a ragged slot barely six feet wide, its depth unknowable. Behind this igneous dam, the Stikine roiled and churned in a giant cauldron, thrusting all its power to find escape. Eddy walls writhed like snakes, currents abruptly reversed direction, boils pushed his boat upward, then dropped beneath him like elevators.

Doug drove his boat into the current flowing directly through the slot and summoned up one last concentrated effort to resist the buffeting, to maintain his momentum and direction. The width of the slot was much less than a boat length, and to get thrown into it sideways would be catastrophic. He rode up onto the pillow of water, straining to reach the slot, felt the current commit him to the narrow passage. The polished black walls shot past, and, suddenly, like emerging from some dark and violent underworld, he floated in a vast, still pool, fifty yards across and teeming with millions of tiny bubbles, bursting all around him, whispering.

We made it. No more obstacles. We're free to go home. To the sea. To Robin.

Waves of emotion engulfed him as he paddled fifteen miles of the lower river to the only road access, almost oblivious to a punishing cold headwind that numbed his hands on the paddle and drained his depleted energy reserves. Hysterical screams into the sky, fists pounding on the boat, as he realized that it was over, that he had done it, that he was alive. An overwhelming sense of accomplishment, of having faced and overcome his fears, of having tested the very limits of his body and soul. For the only time in his life, he had set aside all his many passions and obligations to focus on this single goal, to see how far he could take it, and he had found within himself a place few would ever know. Consuming guilt, for his compulsion to briefly forsake Robin and the children to undertake this risk. Awe of the connection he had found to the inanimate powers that shape the Earth. Dread of the reactions he would face from his cherished paddling teammates, who would not understand. And overlaying it all, a deep, bone-weary exhaustion. Riding his bow up onto the beach by the road, he sat for ten minutes, his numbed fingers unable to pry off his neoprene sprayskirt.

Doug called Robin from the nearest telephone, at Dease Lake. Told her he was off the river and safe. Admitted what he had just done.

Once home, Doug printed out several snapshots from the canyon and put them up on his home office wall, but after a couple of days he took them all down. All the fears from the night at the put-in came flooding back each time he looked at them. That door he had kept closed by sheer willpower would now burst open onto vivid flashes of the instant of losing control, of the rock about to strike him, of getting wedged underwater by unseen hazards. Flashbacks to events that never happened.

Then, as winter rains enveloped Missoula and the snowline edged daily lower, a recurring nightmare replaced the phantom flashbacks. He is in a dark, windswept place, with rain and wet rock and a roar like the river or a high wind in the trees. Something unseen is aware of him, focused on him, pursuing him — relentless, cold, and infinitely powerful. Repeatedly, he turns to face it, and always it eludes him, coming closer, the threat growing unbearably. He knows he cannot escape it, knows he must fight it to the death, knows he cannot win.

He hit Robin in one of those desperate nocturnal struggles, and he had to sleep in another bed for months. Awake, he was the same gentle, loving husband and father to their children that he had always been. Asleep, now, he was a powerful martial artist, and neither Doug nor Robin knew what else. Only then did Robin begin to understand how far he had been, when he phoned from the road to tell her he had finished his river trip and was coming home.

Over time the nightmares became less frequent and less violent. But the nameless, formless horror continued to haunt his dreams, especially in the fall — Stikine season.

Years later he came across a book about spirits in the mythologies of various cultures. As he flipped a page, suddenly, with a déjà vu that snatched his breath like a kick in the stomach, he knew he was staring directly at the nameless, faceless nemesis that stalked his dreams. The Algonquin tribes of North America knew it as a wendigo, a manitou or spirit of the bleak winters in the vast subarctic, the famine times. They depicted it in various forms, most often as a huge, gaunt semi-human figure with the head of an antlered animal and the large glistening eyes of that other silent hunter of the winter nights, the owl. Conjured up by intense isolation and stress, it pursued its victims, often through their dreams, with animal cunning and irresistible power. It could turn men into cannibals, transform them into its own image, separate them irrevocably from tribe and clan and family.

This manifestation from the dark side of Doug's experience did not negate his equally overwhelming sense of accomplishment: of having faced and overcome his fears, of having tested his limits, of having touched the planet in a profound and mysterious way. Some twenty years after his return from the Stikine, Doug was again in Dease Lake. A close paddling friend had died on the river, and Doug spent a long, emotional night talking with a friend and his wife, the daughter of a First Nations Tahltan chief, about the meaning of the canyon to the Tahltan — and to Doug.

Just before the hint of false dawn, he described to them his sudden compulsion, that first night alone in the canyon, to immerse himself naked in the cold river, in the surging cleft between giant boulders, to feel the river shaking the entire canyon, and to sense the enveloping, consuming earth.

After long moments, the Tahltan chieftain's daughter said softly, "Thank you for praying in that place."

CHAPTER TEN

As Yet Unknown

The Yarlung Tsangpo River

At the same time that we are earnest to explore and learn
all things, we require that all things be mysterious and
unexplorable, that land and sea be infinitely wild
— HENRY DAVID THOREAU

Spring 2022, Lexington, Virginia
I sit at my desk and watch spring engulf the Virginia Blue Ridge
outside my window. At a distance, across my horizon, the redbud and
dogwood and mountain laurel, the dark pines, the weathered limestone and granite roots of the ancient mountain range, all fade into
denim pastels. These gentle contours are the heart of my "older and
wiser" mountains, the Appalachians, whose serpentine river valleys
nurtured Tom McEwan and myself from the moment we met in a
grade school lunchroom and discovered a mutual passion for rivers,
and have continued to do so across six decades.

In stark contrast, beside that window hangs a map. Amoebas of
glacial white sprawl across the landscape reach arms deep into chasms
brown with tightly packed contour lines and truncate into zigzag veins
of blue. No reds of cities, towns, or roads. In an attempt to organize the
chaos, twenty-five years ago I superimposed black arrows and neatly
printed labels: a put-in; landmarks and remote villages, rendezvous
points for resupply; and primary and alternate takeouts. Tom and I
were preparing to plunge deep into the youngest, most savage mountains on the planet, where the Yarlung Tsangpo River bores through
the eastern end of the Himalayas in the ancient yin and yang of water

and rock: the colliding continents that thrust mountains miles into the sky, and the steady flow of ice and water that rends their flanks and tears them down with every drop from the monsoon-laden sky. A reincarnation of what my Blue Ridge would have been a half-billion years ago.

October 5, 1998, Pei, Tibet

The Himalayas deceive even the most experienced explorers and mountaineers when they first encounter its unearthly scales, its grandeur, and its terror. Tom McEwan, his brother Jamie McEwan, Roger Zbel, and Doug Gordon knew this full well, expected no less. They knew too that the Tsangpo River before them was still swollen from much greater than normal monsoon rains the past summer. At the final road access before it roared into its great horseshoe bend around the eastern end of the Himalayan range, it flowed slick and brown and fast between sandbanks and river-polished rock. And wide, very wide. "It is going to be very big rapids down there," Jamie recorded in his journal. "And this, of course, is the easy part."

From road's end at the village of Pei to Gyala, fifteen miles downstream, would serve as the team's warm-up — and decision maker. Here the gradient was much less than they would encounter farther in. Terraces of cultivation and the smoke of cookfires added human scale to the surrounding valley. A well-traveled footpath above the right bank connected the two villages and would allow a support team of Harry and Doris Wetherbee, Nepalese Sherpa Pemba, and *National Geographic* videographer Paulo Castillo to parallel the river team with local porters, resupply them at Gyala, or pull them back out if farther progress downstream was not possible. The river team would reaccustom to their boats and moving water after their flight halfway around the world and days of punishing driving overland from Kathmandu, around Mount Everest, and through Lhasa to finally arrive at the put-in. They would, after months of rumor and speculation, actu-

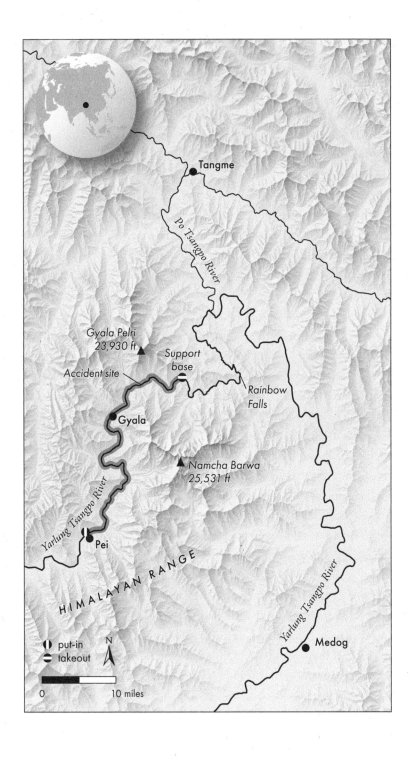

Tangme

Po Tsangpo River

Gyala Pelri
23,930 ft

Support
base

Accident site

Rainbow
Falls

Gyala

Namcha Barwa
25,531 ft

Yarlung Tsangpo River

Pei

HIMALAYAN RANGE

Yarlung Tsangpo River

Medog

put-in
takeout

N

0   10 miles

ally evaluate the flooded river and, critically, its daily drop in volume. They would shake down their equipment under actual conditions.

Above all, Tom believed, they must use these all important first days to find their rhythm as a team and with this river. Ahead lay the biggest river challenge any of them had ever faced. Success could only come with flawless teamwork among the four paddlers and also with the support crews essential to their resupply — and perhaps their rescue. They would take several days, test themselves on the water, and at Gyala make their decision. From there they could cut the first support team umbilical and continue into the unknown canyon on their own, to rendezvous and resupply some twenty-five miles downstream with myself, team medic Dave Phillips, mountain guide and Tibetan linguist Ang Kami Sherpa from Kathmandu, and local Monpa hunters.

Or they could make the perhaps more difficult decision: that it was not a go, that this was not the year, that they were not the team. None of the four knew, as they stepped into their boats and tobogganed twenty feet down a steep sandbank into the surging brown water, how that decision would go. They knew, though, that for them Gyala was the place to make it. Not earlier, at the expedition assembly point in McLean, Virginia, based upon satellite photos and news reports weeks in advance, nor in Lhasa, based on a single glimpse of the river miles upstream and the observations of strangers. The Tsangpo and its soaring canyon walls would provide the cold, hard facts behind their choice.

Meanwhile, they had a river to run. Jamie shot out into the current first, felt it welling up and accelerating beneath his hull, hurtling him downstream to the first wave train, an open roller coaster of pulsing waves, their tops intermittently piling too steep and breaking like combers at sea. Almost too late, he realized the trap the Himalayas set even for those forewarned. The swiftly approaching waves were enormous, their unpredictable breaking tops big enough to engulf him and his boat, to throw him end over end, pound him back into the wave's trough at the water's mercy. He powered toward the left bank, coasted past the maelstrom.

Not so Doug. Perched on shore beside the rapid with his camera, Jamie watched Doug sail up over the center of the first big wave, plunge down into the trough behind, and disappear into the breaking second wave. The white crest seemed to tumble forever, and Jamie was convinced Doug must be out of his boat when he finally saw the blue hull wash out downstream. Relief as Doug began to roll up turned to further dismay as he was knocked back down, repeatedly. Torn loose from the bracing inside his boat, he was not able to reposition and upright himself until his third attempt. Doug drifted out of Jamie's sight downriver, unhurt but chastened. Tom and Roger paddled a conservative route down the right shore.

This was the transition day, a day to regain their focus and their muscle memory of the water. They paddled with lightweight, empty boats, their gear at the launch point base camp, and they ran one rapid multiple times, for practice and for the cameras. The brilliant ice fields of the Namcha Barwa massif gleamed among puffy white cumulus in a glorious blue sky.

The warm-up and the photography were necessary, Tom admitted to himself, but after the first day he was determined to make the run down to Gyala a full-on dress rehearsal. The gradient of the river was less than it would be beyond, and the hillsides not as steep, but they would henceforth paddle with a full load of river gear and bivouac at river level. The Wetherbees and the support team were to parallel their route on the trail high above the right bank, but the two teams would only connect again, and the river team resupply, in Gyala. This too was a scaled-down exercise of the way they hoped to proceed downriver: legs of roughly ten days Alpine-style, self-contained and agile, able to maneuver from one side of the river to the other. Then they would rendezvous with siege-style support teams, porters bringing them supplies and replacement equipment.

Cut loose from the support team, its train of porters, the nagging complications of logistics and personalities, and the incessant intrusion of locals into their personal space and time, the four focused with relief on the river and the task they had come to accomplish; days of powerful rapids and even more difficult scrambling across steep cliffs to scout ahead; nights of campfires on sand beaches, hot high-calorie meals, cocooned in their Gore-Tex bivouac sacks. From their first bivouac, Tom was scheduled to record an interview with National Public Radio via satellite phone. It had to be postponed; he could not be heard over the roar of the river. Each day brought a better appreciation of the huge landscape that engulfed them.

Balancing his boat on a boulder of river-worn, black-and-white gneiss, Jamie slid into the bracing and prepared to seal-launch into a surging eddy below. His brother Tom tipped forward from his own rock, splashed awkwardly, then stroked smoothly downstream to an eddy where he waited for Jamie to join him. Then, as Jamie reached forward to seal his spray deck onto the cockpit rim, his entire future on the expedition evaporated in an instant. His minuscule change of weight unbalanced the boat, which plunged from its rocky perch into the river below, gallons of water pouring unchecked into the open cockpit. Bracing furiously with his paddle to keep the wallowing boat upright, he drifted downstream, yet more water pouring in with each pulse of the river.

Directly ahead, a mammoth rock split the channel like the prow of a ship, to its left the safety of the shore, to its right the main river — which they had not yet scouted. Jamie, his boat by now almost completely awash, turned over, and when he rolled up he could see that the approaching prow of the rock had no "bone in its teeth," no cushion of water rebounding where rock and water collided. The rock was undercut! The powerful current could trap him underneath with escape or rescue nearly impossible. Now fearing for his life, he kicked forcefully out of the boat. That propelled him away from the fateful undercut, but at a price. The boat and all his gear disappeared out into the main current. Flashes of bright sunlight and shining mountains alternated with cold and murky water, and fear commingled with an odd sense of relief. His individual responsibility, his desperate struggle to salvage the situation after his own careless act, was over. He was now flotsam in the river's grip, his immediate task simply to breathe. Even that required an intimate partnership with the massive river. He felt the rhythm of the waves, gasped deep lungfuls of air at each crest, tried to avoid choking as he was again engulfed.

A flash of blue and orange, his brother's kayak, and of black, the nylon grab loop at its stern. "Jamie, grab hold," Tom shouted over the river's roar. Powerful strokes ferried them both to the safety of a shoreline eddy. Jamie released his grip on his brother's stern, swam the remaining few feet, and, using his paddle as a staff, staggered over wet, slippery rocks to dry land. Turning, he shouted to his brother that he was fine, waved him off, and implored him to pursue the lost boat. Tom took a few hesitant strokes downstream, but at the bottom of the eddy he broke off and returned. He would have followed to rescue Jamie himself, as Mike Jones did for Roger Huyton on the Braldu in 1979, but no equipment was worth chasing into that unknown.

Aware that the combination of cold-water shock and adrenaline surge often make a whitewater accident victim the last to realize their condition, Tom repeatedly asked Jamie if he was okay, if he was warm enough, if he was injured. Standing dripping on the shore, Jamie was in equal measure distraught over the loss of his boat and grateful for the solicitude of his often-remote older brother. It sometimes seemed that only on the rivers could the two bridge the five-year divide in ages that had loomed so large in childhood, and which never quite went away.

Like tiny water bugs, red and blue on the brown river roughly a thousand feet below, Jamie saw his three former companions pull out on a sand beach on the far shore and start to make camp for the night. The walkie-talkie clipped to his yellow life vest came alive, and Doug's disembodied voice crackled in the still air. "River team to Jamie. River team to Jamie. Come in, please." Tom, Doug, and Roger were within sight and sound, yet their separation was insurmountable. Lost along with his boat was his part on that team, participation in the greatest expedition of their lives. Gone too were his journals and exposed film — records of everything he had accomplished so far. Washing down into the maw of the Tsangpo Gorge was a symbol of all the boats on all the rivers that, along with his family, defined his life: his two Olympics, the Bronze medal, expeditions to Bhutan and Mexico with Tom and me, wilderness runs in the Canadian Rockies with Doug. Thousands of hours chasing whitewater dreams.

Sourly he turned and resumed his solitary trek to join the support team in Gyala. Unbidden, a mantra formed and replayed in his mind. *Do nothing. Be no one.* Jamie had no idea what it meant, but it persisted.

From wooden poles twenty feet high, tall white prayer flags flapped their messages heavenward along the footpath entering Gyala, and today they delivered a miracle. Jamie's lost boat had been found in a huge eddy on the left a couple of miles downstream. Even his dry bags of gear had survived and had been recovered, an SLR camera the sole loss. An afternoon of high diplomacy and negotiating drama followed, and by the time Tom, Doug, and Roger paddled ashore at camp that evening they were again a full river team of four. But to what end? Downstream, the jaws of Nanga Parbat and Gyala Pelri closed in on the swollen river, and now was decision time.

Just as its layered beds of fossiliferous limestones thrust the geologic history of the Earth a mile into the air, so too humans have layered centuries of legend, faith, and history within the gorge. Aboriginal tribes migrating from Bhutan and elsewhere, Buddhist saints and pilgrims, spies of the British Raj, Chinese Red Guards, and Western explorers have all in their turn sought various nirvanas in its depths.

For a thousand years, yogis and lama adepts of Tantric Buddhism have sought, in the inaccessible folds of these mountains, the greatest of all the world's *beyuls*, magically hidden valleys where the physical and spiritual worlds overlap. More than the geomorphology of the restless planet Earth, this hidden land of Pemakö was also a living, sacred landscape, its mountains and valleys physical manifestations of a supine Tantric goddess, Dorji Phagmo.

Pemakö is not, however, to be mistaken for a Christian paradise nor for the hidden utopia of Hollywood's *Lost Horizon*. On the contrary; it is a world of incessant hardship and danger, where the pilgrim is poised between death and enlightenment. In the words of Buddhist scholar and explorer Ian Baker, "Only by recognizing your insecurities, when you're confronting death, do you see the nature of life, self, and reality. In that regard Pemakö is paradise. The misconception that it's heaven on earth is one that even Tibetans have had. In different periods, they've gone to Pemakö searching for an earthly paradise and found instead a terrifying place full of tigers and wild savages. It wasn't the paradise they had in mind."

If any of the seekers actually traveled the full length of the gorge in the physical sense, they left only cryptic hints that baffled even the most exalted gurus.

The quest was different for explorers, cartographers, and spies of the British Raj in the late nineteenth and early twentieth centuries, although they too encountered the tigers and savages, unscalable cliffs and unfordable rivers, leeches, rain, and snow. The Tsangpo River was known to flow eastward across Tibet, at an elevation of more than nine thousand feet, into the knot of mountains at the eastern end of the Himalayas, where it disappeared from Western geographers' ken. Which of the great rivers of South and Southeast Asia was its downstream terminus — the Brahmaputra, the Irrawaddy, the Salween, or even the Mekong — and what happened during that missing link of thousands of feet of elevation? The Tsangpo was one of the great geographical puzzles of the late nineteenth century.

First to tackle the problem were the Pundits, foot soldiers on the front lines of Kipling's Great Game. As immortalized in *Kim*, the Pundits were natives recruited from the frontiers of the Indian Empire and trained by the Great Trigonometrical Survey to conduct clandestine surveys into unknown lands beyond the borders of British India to forestall surprise threats from a rapidly expanding and increasingly bellicose czarist Russia. Disguised as pilgrims, merchants, and other innocent travelers, on arduous foot journeys that often lasted years, and under threat of death if detected, they paced off distances counting on special Buddhist (or Muslim) strings of prayer beads, calculated the altitude of mountain passes from the boiling temperature of their tea water measured with thermometers concealed in hollowed-out walking sticks, and recorded coded field notes among the paper prayers within their prayer wheels.

One of the greatest of these clandestine servants of the Raj was an unassuming tailor from Sikkim named Kintup. His mission, in 1880, was simply to follow the course of the Tsangpo River from Tibet to the sea, to prove once and for all where it debouched. As for those before and since, the task was not, in fact, simple. Kintup traveled in the guise of a servant to his assigned partner, a lama, and when the unscrupulous holy man sold him into slavery and disappeared into the night with all their operational funds, Kintup could not deny his servant status without blowing his cover. Instead, he endured months of slavery, and when he managed to escape, loyal Kintup fled not back to India but downstream to continue his mission, his outraged purchasers in full pursuit. He was finally forced to abandon the mission, not by the slave-hunting Tibetans but by xenophobic headhunters in the jungles of northeast India. And when he ultimately made his way home, after four years "missing in action," came the final indignity: The British officers who had dispatched him had rotated back to England, and the incumbents disbelieved his amazing tale.

The quest for the Tsangpo was taken up by intrepid British early in the twentieth century. Legendary British political officer F. M. Bailey, who had accompanied Francis Younghusband's expedition to subject Tibet in 1903–1904, and who would later conduct daring espionage operations behind Bolshevik lines during World War I, made his way upstream from the Brahmaputra and past the headhunters, only to be stymied, as Kintup had been, by the savage mountain topography below Gyala. Close on his heels, in 1924–1925, followed another legend of Asian exploration, plant collector F. Kingdon Ward. Ranging the lush mountain slopes of Yunnan, China, and eastern Tibet, Kingdon Ward spent most of his life collecting exotic plant specimens for commercial nurseries in Great Britain. When he worked his way into the last remaining few miles of the gorge unknown to Western geographers, though, he was equally intent on chasing down rumors of a huge waterfall, to rival Niagara or Victoria, hidden in the mysterious depths.

Kingdon Ward concluded, however, that there was no single, giant waterfall, writing:

> There is a legend current amongst the Tibetans, and said to be recorded in certain sacred books kept in the monastery at Pemakochung, that between the rainbow fall and the confluence there are no less than seventy-five of these falls, each presided over by a spirit — whether benevolent or malicious is not stated. Supposing that to be more or less true, and supposing each fall or rapid to be only 20 feet high, the difference of height is easily accounted for.

Fifty-eight years later in 1983, that description captured the dreams of Tom McEwan and myself. Freshly returned from an exploratory in Bhutan, and seeking "what next," for us the Tsangpo, with its supreme whitewater challenges, its history and romance, seemed the ultimate grail. And if Kingdon Ward's description was correct, agile kayaks might be the perfect tool to complete the mission that eluded every explorer on foot. Not all twenty-foot waterfalls or drops would be runnable, of course, but we had run many, and rappelled as many more.

Tom and I were not alone in our Tsangpo dreams. As with the Yangtze, from around the world explorers and adventurers began to circle as the Chinese emerged from their long isolation. And just as with the Yangtze, the Chinese were determined to extract substantial permit fees for a major whitewater expedition on their "Mount

Everest of rivers." First in were smaller exploratories, primarily on
foot, in the early 1990s: *National Geographic's* David Breashears
and Gordon Wiltsie, Arizona canyoneer* Richard Fisher, Buddhist
scholar Ian Baker, explorers Gil and Troy Gillenwater, and others.
Japanese survivalist Yoshitaka Takei and a companion trekked down
the tributary Po Tsangpo with two kayaks and launched onto the
middle section of the gorge. Both capsized immediately; Takei was
never recovered.

By 1997 plans were under way for several major whitewater expeditions. From Germany, Lucas Blücher was pulling together a strong
international team of kayakers, including Doug Ammons from
Montana. American international rafting outfitter Steve Currey was
raising money for a major effort. That spring filmmaker and expedition kayaker Scott Lindgren and Charlie Munsey did a short exploratory, kayaking part of the Po Tsangpo route into the middle gorge,
and in October, Tom McEwan, Harry and Doris Wetherbee, and I
trekked into the gorge to see the legendary river firsthand and evaluate
the feasibility of an expedition in the fall of 1998.

Could they, or should they, continue downstream, and if so, how?
Tom, Jamie, Doug, and Roger confronted the crux decision of the
entire expedition on the white sand beach that encompassed their
base camp below Gyala as they waited for the return of Jamie's lost-
and-found boat. They had known from their first glimpse of the
flood-swollen river far upstream that their original goal of traversing seventy or more miles through the Tsangpo Gorge was not to
be, had perhaps always been overly optimistic. Now, with few of the
major rapids runnable, fewer routes on land near river level, and fewer
places to cross the main flow to the opposite shore, each mile down-

* Merriam-Webster defines *canyoneering* as "the sport of exploring canyons (as by
climbing, rappelling, or rafting)."

stream would demand time-and-energy-consuming bushwhacking and climbing, much of it with mountaineering equipment — if it were even possible.

Risk is inherent in whitewater exploration. Just the year prior Doug had written, following the river death of fellow US team member Richie Weiss, "The joy, the satisfaction, the personal growth I've experienced through paddling and the spectacular places I've seen are well worth the risk. But let's not pretend that the risk isn't there. It's there and it's very real and if we don't do everything we can to deal with it and minimize it, then we've missed a very important lesson."

The warm-up run from Pei to Gyala had demonstrated that here risk lay not just in the size and power of the water but also in the care demanded for every move, every footstep, every encounter with the unforgiving landscape — the river and side streams, the rocks, the wildlife, and even the vegetation. In the narrow margins between success and catastrophe, even a minor injury or loss of critical equipment could frustrate years of planning and training. Now each paddler needed to reach deep into his lifetime of experience and weigh his personal goals both on the river and off as well as his gut feel from the last five days. And the four then needed to reach consensus on the team goal and how to achieve it.

Jamie was unenthused. If the choice were entirely his, he confided in his journal, he would probably hang it up and go home to his family. They had come to run a river. If that was now going to morph into endless bushwhacking and rock climbing, he would sooner not tackle it. But that was a vote he would lose, he wrote, so he said nothing. He was there to be a team player.

Roger was conservative. On joining the expedition, he had determined that his uncompromising goal was to remain safe, to return to his family and his rafting company in Maryland, and, despite his skills and experience running flooded rivers in the United States, to portage anything that presented even the risk of capsize. However, of them all he was also the most confident overland. With his burly frame and stoic endurance, he could hang his boat full of supplies and equipment on his shoulder and cover miles in almost any terrain.

Doug was pragmatic. They were in perhaps the most exotic, least explored canyon on Earth, and he was determined to see it, taste it, smell it, experience it in every possible way. He believed that success would come from balancing caution with boldness, from forging ahead and not becoming bogged down. That was what Alpine style was all about. He was also aware that he was probably the boldest paddler of the four, but he resolved not to let his choices influence the others.

Tom was determined to lead by example, and from the middle, not the front. They had learned some lessons, begun to gel as a team, and gained some comfort on the water during their test run from Pei to Gyala. He did not feel they yet had that mysterious rhythm with one another, with the canyon walls, and with the river that would enable at least limited success. But with each day they gained more — and the river level dropped.

Four strong minds, and decades of devotion to the rivers and mountains that shape the planet.

As the entire future of our expedition hung with that decision, I was miles to the north, on the opposite flank of Mount Gyala Pelri, and linked to the rest of the expedition only by tenuous satellite telephone reports. This was deliberate. Tom and I had conceived this project fifteen years before, planned in detail, flown halfway around the world to scout the previous year; obtained sponsorship from *National Geographic*, Polartec, Space Imaging, and others; formed the river and support elements, and driven across the Tibetan Plateau to get here. But the decision of whether to go into the gorge, and if so how, was not mine to make — nor to influence, even unintentionally.

So at a fork in the long road from Lhasa, our teams had split. The paddlers and the Wetherbee support team rolled south, to the put-in at Pei and the decision point at Gyala. Dave Phillips and I split off north to find our way overland to the first resupply point, roughly twenty-five miles downstream from the put-in but sixty road miles and ten days' trekking to get there. Standing beside the dusty road, our truck drivers gunning their engines and belching black diesel smoke in their impatience to get on to the next tea stop, I had voiced to Tom my discomfort with this necessary separation. It felt as if I were abandoning my leadership role. Tom smiled, lips tight, as if leaving things unsaid. It was the right choice, he told me gently.

"Boat-assisted hiking," Doug dubbed it. The team re-sorted their gear one last time, added extra food, and plunged into the gorge. They expected mostly climbing along the shores, but they would test the premise that their boats would allow some flexibility in crossing from bank to bank — an advantage none of the previous explorers over the centuries had enjoyed. Their available time and energy might at most allow them to penetrate the roughly twenty-five miles to Rainbow Falls, their first planned resupply point. It seemed likely they might have to abandon the boats at some point and make their way solely on foot. Either way, they would experience the grandest of all canyons, including that magical, invisible point directly between the peaks of Namcha Barwa and Gyala Pelri, where canyon walls towered more than sixteen thousand feet above the river. Tom noticed that the water level at the first rapid had dropped four inches overnight.

Before they cut contact with the support team, however, they paused at the first rapid below the town, a big wave train with a trail beside it, which they dubbed the Video Rapid. They coasted down the edges of the huge waves as Paulo filmed from shore — his last opportunity to film the paddlers. Doug experimented with a helmet-mounted "lipstick" video camera, and Tom mounted a *National Geographic*–supplied still camera to a bracket on his bow. Here again, the scale of the Himalayas confounded best estimates — this time of the professional photographers and engineers at NGS headquarters. The Nikon diver's camera on Tom's bow was rigged with a remote control so a photographer on shore could snap the pictures while Tom paddled the kayak. But here, the route down the huge river, even when avoiding the center, was beyond the range of the remote control. Unwilling to accept such a technological setback, Doug duct-taped the remote to his paddle shaft and paddled behind Tom, triggering the camera.

As the water dropped, the nearly continuous, powerful rapids would become separated by pools, but for the moment paddling in the powerful main channel remained out of the question, and places to safely ferry from one shore to the other were rare. Their cautious progress down the left shore came to a halt as both shorelines steepened and a series of huge holes and gargantuan exploding waves shot geysers of spume twenty feet into the air before slamming into a cliff several hundred yards beyond.

From a safe crossing above the monster the team split into pairs to explore both sides for a way around. Doug and Jamie worked along the steepening left bank, their movements synchronized with barely a word after two recent expeditions in the wilderness Rockies of British Columbia and thousands of hours of pushing each other to new levels in slalom training. Across the river, Roger and Tom paralleled down the right bank, their movements not as intuitive as Doug's and Jamie's, but their partnership was forged both by years of companionship and rivalry in downriver racing in the Appalachians and in Europe, and now by their converging approach to the Tsangpo.

The cliffs before Doug and Jamie became increasingly difficult, but Tom and Roger found a route on the right to a point where they could launch below the big rapid and paddle down the right shoreline. Rejoined, they wrestled their loaded boats across the portage, only to discover their route down the right side "cliffed out" less than a mile downstream. They could go no farther by boat, and a climb around would be at least a twelve-hundred-foot ascent, with no telling where or what the descent would then be like.

A sand beach above the river became their bivouac for the night, a place to recuperate for the test to come. Whatever the enormous physical demands and emotional stresses of their days, Tom found, there was equal comfort and relief in each night's camp: warm, high-calorie meals, comforting wood fires, snug sleeping bags. He believed that a person could endure almost anything if provided enough fuel and sleep for nightly recovery. He wondered, sometimes, about his younger brother staying up long past dark, talking with Doug or writing in his journal by headlamp. Recovery could take different forms.

A backbreaking retreat up the shoreline, to where they had crossed so hopefully the day before, consumed the morning. Caching the boats on the left shore, and carrying only bivouac gear, two days' rations, and their rudimentary climbing kit, the four climbed up a side stream roaring down from the glaciers of Gyala Pelri, seeking the route downstream that had eluded Doug and Jamie. That evening was dry and firewood plentiful, so Jamie built a larger, more cheerful fire than usual. It took them all the following day to forge a way down the left flank to the next place they could cross the river, then to return to their cached boats. They were at exactly the point where they had started three days before.

Jamie knew that Doug was frustrated with the lack of progress. More retreats like they had just experienced would eat up their time and supplies — would break them. He admired Doug's restraint, his calm acceptance of the group's conservative choices.

Festina lente. Make haste slowly. Tom counseled patience. They had learned the next lesson: It was not sufficient to scout ahead just enough to be sure they could retreat if necessary. They must also explore ahead to the next safe crossing before committing. A "global scout," Tom noted in his journal.

An entire day hauling the laden boats down the left with ropes and pulleys was followed by an exhilarating day of mixed paddling and climbing portages. They made an idyllic camp that evening on a grassy shelf overlooking the sweeping river two hundred feet below. It was easier to talk, back from the constant roar of the Tsangpo, and the air hung heavy with pine. The day had been "a little of everything" according to Doug, their best since departing Gyala. After days of retreat and uncertainty, they were again moving purposely downstream. Tom felt much of the team's frustration drain away and his own leadership

burden lighten. If tomorrow went as well, he would try to get back
to filming with the little digital videocam *National Geographic* had
supplied.

At their evening satellite telephone check, Tom cut loose from the
Wetherbee support team and committed the river team downstream.
The Wetherbees had been waiting between Gyala and Pei, poised to
hike back into the gorge if the paddlers needed assistance retreating
back upstream. They would now loop around by truck, ready to assist
farther down.

That same evening culminated a day of rest and feasting for Dave,
myself, Ang Kami Sherpa, and our Monpa porter guides. Roughly ten
miles beyond and thirty-five hundred feet above the river camp, the
Monpas had pursued and shot a takin, a rare wild bovine that best
resembles a blue-eyed musk ox. Only after a day of gorging on the
heart and other bloody organs, then smoking strips of meat over fires
of green rhododendron and rendering the rest into blood sausage to
be picked up on their return journey, did we forge on to our planned
rendezvous with Tom and the team.

The scene was wild, awesome, and, for the Tsangpo, typical. Downstream, the river narrowed and swept directly into a series of six river-
wide recirculating holes, monster trenches of plunging white perhaps
forty yards across and ten to twenty feet in depth. The paddlers leaned
helmet-to-helmet to confer above the thundering river. Close by the
left shore, a narrow rocky channel tumbled down eight or ten vertical feet, too congested for a clean line but an acceptable "sneak route"
to the next eddy nonetheless. One step farther out toward the main
stream, the drop was a single plunge into a recirculating hole somewhat more than a boat length across. It appeared a kayak with speed
could punch through at the corners, but Tom pointed out that the
hole slanted left to right, and that a boat or boater stuck there would
be ejected out toward the center channel.

Tom made his decision quickly and lugged his kayak down the
shore to video. Hastily unpacking his camera, he positioned himself

on a boulder below the drop and focused on Doug's line next to shore. Roger followed, also on foot, and Jamie withheld judgment to see how it went for Doug.

When Doug's boat appeared at the top of the drop, it was not in Tom's viewfinder next to shore but rather on the lip of the direct drop, Doug stroking hard to punch through the left corner of the powerful recirculation below. Tom's surprise that Doug had chosen this route after he and Roger portaged downstream quickly turned to concern. Doug's line from right to left into the corner of the hole appeared good, and at first his boat punched through the foam wall, toward the safety of the downstream current near shore. Then, in agonizing slow motion, and despite Doug's straining pull on his left paddle blade, his momentum stalled, and the kayak slid backward into the maw of the hole. No longer in slow motion, too quickly to count, the stern plunged into the falling water, the kayak flipped end over end, disappeared under the white recirculating water, reemerged in flashes of blue hull, orange life jacket, yellow helmet, for sixteen violent, thrashing seconds.

Keeping the video camera trained on the unfolding action, Tom glanced over his left shoulder. When Doug washed out of the hole on the right, Tom's seventy-foot throw-rope would be useless — the scale of the Tsangpo was far beyond that limit. But there were roughly two hundred feet for Doug to roll up and return to shore before the hellacious holes downstream. Doug had been thrashed in similar situations many times before — tuck, wait for the churning to cease, roll up. For him, this was automatic.

Concern transformed to horror. Doug's three teammates watched in disbelief as the boat finally washed out of the right corner of the hole, and three times Doug's efforts to roll failed. Like a novice, he would come partway up, gasp for air, and fall back upside down. They watched, helpless, as the blue hull swept downstream, to river center, then disappeared into the first of the monstrous, unforgiving holes. After long seconds that seemed like hours, they saw a flash of blue in the second hole. And in the third. Then nothing.

Tom knew from that moment that there was no hope, that they had witnessed Doug's death, that everything had changed. They had no choice, though, but to pelt downstream, to search and attempt a rescue, no matter how improbable. Abandoning their boats, Tom and Roger raced down the left shore. Jamie ripped out his gear bags, shouldered his empty boat and followed, alternately portaging and paddling — who knew where he might have to go in search of his best friend. He scouted from his boat, ran drops he should not have, swore he would not do that again. His meticulously kept journal was blank for three days, and of that fugue he later recalled:

> The sun was just setting . . . with the sun shining in from one side, through the gorge. The world seemed to have picked up the feelings inside me and was painting them across the enormous landscape with majestic and unearthly light, a light like the sound of violins, mountains like drums, river like horns and cymbals and trumpets . . . Slowly, step by step, in the huge aloneness, I waded the glacier-cold stream. I crossed mud and gravel. I moved on into undergrowth threaded with low takin trails. I climbed up and down small cliffs to search out a better route.
>
> I was just opposite the whirlpool-infested pool when I heard Doug's voice shout "Jamie!"
>
> The breath went out of me. I forced my way out of the bushes to the edge of a fifteen-foot escarpment and looked down on the rocks lining the river below me. The water was flowing upstream, in a large circular eddy moving up as fast as most rivers ever flow down. There were eddies within this eddy, formed by irregularities in the bank. Breathing hard, I looked up and down. No one.
>
> I moved back and forth around the bushes, for a better view. Finally I found a way down the escarpment and searched among the rocks. Nothing.
>
> I listened. The river was making a number of distinct sounds. Hissing along the rocks. Slurping on the eddy line. Plopping

and clopping farther out. A chorus, from upstream and down, of rolling churning roars that came from a host of recirculating holes and endlessly breaking waves. Thumps as uprearing waves fell back upon themselves. Surf against the shoreline rocks. Out of these sounds I could almost hear human sounds form: incoherent shouts, mutterings, a babble of proto-voices. These must have fooled me. I searched awhile longer, and then gave up . . .

During the next days . . . I heard more voices, though never Doug's again. I heard a chorus of children singing; snatches of conversation; shouts and exclamations, all formed from the chaos of surging water sounds, and melding back into river sounds again. It was eerie, startling, and oddly comforting. A reminder that all of civilized life was still going on somewhere, waiting for our return.

Ironically, as Tom, Jamie, and Roger forged their way downstream, in their urgency and grief, searching vainly for Doug, they finally found their full rhythm with the gorge. Knowing that they must scout a route ahead all the way to the next safe crossing point before proceeding with their boats, they now scouted ahead packing most of their supplies and equipment, then returned to run the river or navigate the canyon walls with empty boats. With his blond Viking beard, his stocky frame and stolid endurance, like some Himalayan bear, Roger leaned into the task, finding routes, hacking through the underbrush, selecting campsites. They passed a glacier from Gyala Pelri poking all the way down to the river, a silty brown tongue of meltwater emerging from its cavernous snout. They passed the invisible "deepest point," more than sixteen thousand feet below the peaks of Namcha Barwa and Gyala Pelri. For three days they made steady progress — progress that might have curbed Doug's impatience.

The pug marks of a golden leopard crisscrossed the damp sand beach of the base camp Dave and I established with our Monpa guides at river level, eight and a half miles downstream from the accident site, and the gnawed bones of takin and garwal littered cavernous under-cuts beneath a huge, water-polished boulder that now provided our shelter. From this remote, exotic base, we explored the left banks of the Tsangpo, both upstream and down, to be sure we missed no sign of Doug, and we waited to meet the river team to lead our eight-day climb out over formidable terrain.

Late in the afternoon of October 18, fifty-two hours after Roger had last seen the blue flash of Doug's boat in the lethal rapid, Dave heard a single, unintelligible word over the walkie-talkie he was monitoring. Later, from atop a cliff half a mile upstream, he could hear Tom's weary voice clearly over the river's roar. They were on the far shore, and he could see Ang Kami Sherpa and our Monpa searchers opposite their position. We were reunited for the first time since we had parted on the Lhasa road, the paddlers to circle south to the put-in at Pei and down the river, Dave and me to loop north around Gyala Pelri to make our way by foot to this extraordinary rendezvous.

The following day, under a cold mist condensing to evening rain, we formed a somber semicircle to commemorate Doug before our departure from the gorge. Roger, bulky in fleece and ski cap, stood between the two gaunt McEwan brothers, Jamie wrapped in an olive drab poncho, pale but on his feet for the first time since their arrival at base camp, Tom squinting wearily through rain-smeared glasses. The Monpas ranked behind, rain dripping from their black hair and olive-drab Chinese raincoats, hands clasped in gesture of respect and prayer. The younger ones hung back, enthralled but perhaps fearful of what this invocation of foreign gods might entail. Ang Kami Sherpa stood to one side, hands in pockets, respectful but part of neither culture. He had seen death in the mountains many times. Before us, from behind house-sized boulders glistening pink and black in the rain and spray, white spume shot high above our heads. To our left, three-foot waves pulsed up a cobbled beach like ocean surf.

Tom's soft tenor somehow rode above the tumult of the river:

Morning has broken, like the first morning,
Blackbird has spoken, like the first bird,
Praise for the new day, praise for the morning,
God's re-creation of the first day.

The Victorian-era gospel invoked for Tom the early mountain mornings Doug had loved so well. Looking back up the cloud-choked valley, toward the accident site, he intoned a short, extemporaneous prayer for Doug's wife, Connie, and their young sons, Tyler and Bryce.

Two of the Monpa leaders continued the ceremony, placing before the silent group a block of limestone about fourteen inches high, upon which Tom had written Doug's name in black. Taking from under their shirts the 108-bead Buddhist rosaries they wore like necklaces, they began to chant a rhythmic mantra that seemed to echo the backbeat of the river. A couple of the younger Monpas fetched smoldering brands from the fire; another sprinkled on them tsampa* flour to produce a dense and pungent smoke. When the chanting and the smoke tapered off, Tom gestured for the younger Monpas to assemble. In Tibetan they began to sing a melodic folk song, "Yarlung Tsangpo," about the river and homeland and homesickness.

Tom and I stared regretfully downstream, where the nose of a great glacier from Namcha Barwa emerged from the mist and almost reached the swift river. Never had the Tsangpo abyss seemed more remote, or more sublime. Somewhere in the past few days — at terrible cost — the paddlers had finally found that elusive accord with the inhuman forces of the Tsangpo that Tom had sought from their first launch at Pei. Having come so far, to this lonely beach, the last nine miles to complete the first leg of their journey at the Rainbow Falls felt almost within grasp.

---

* A staple Tibetan foodstuff made from roasted barley (and sometimes wheat).

It was not to be. Each of us was by now showing some physical reaction, Jamie's the most severe. His frantic three-day search down the river had been the most desperate, the loss of his closest friend the most staggering blow. Finally, at our base and with hope abandoned, his resistance collapsed after days of adrenaline and tension. Roger helped him rig their tarpaulin over a sandy spot thirty feet away from the busy, communal camp under the rock, and he retreated into his bivvy bag with fever, nausea, and stomach cramps, emerging only to retch periodically.

Himself suffering from painfully bruised ribs from a fall, and twenty pounds lighter than when we had entered the gorge, Dave made his medical rounds, treating American, Sherpa, and Monpa alike: seeing that Jamie took in ample fluids and treating infections on Roger's hands, boils on Ang Kami's back, infected leech bites on Monpa ankles.

More powerful than these physical limitations, however, was the fact that Doug had himself dictated our decision. For the first time in my paddling experience, in Kathmandu I had raised the difficult subject of what should be done if we experienced a fatality. As the others struggled to compose their thoughts, Doug, with his characteristic logic and clarity, already had his answer formed. "That's easy, at least for me. If I were the person to die, leave me there; and if someone dies, get to the nearest exit point . . . I don't think I could go on . . . I just wouldn't — nah, I'd just feel like I ought to be home, talking to that person's family, doing something other than paddling whitewater, having fun."

We would begin our climb out of the gorge in the morning.

Two years after our return from the Yarlung Tsangpo, Jamie McEwan wrote:

I now realize that I do want to go back to Tibet. I even want to launch once more onto the Tsangpo. Why? Just to be there.

I doubt that I will really return. But, strangely, I appreciate the renewed desire. It connects today's self with the one that set forth with my friends in October of 1998.

He, we, did not return. Greek philosopher Heraclitus was correct that no one ever steps in the same river twice, for it's not the same river and they're not the same person. Jamie passed in 2015, and those of us still here, my companions on the Tsangpo and others from the preceding chapters, face the inevitable limits to our physical abilities of twenty-five and more years ago. Moreover, the ancient cycles of freeze and thaw, flood and earthquake, uplift and erosion, have resculpted our canyons even in the human scale of decades.

Anthropocene humans too redesign the planet in their image at an ever-increasing pace. Buses of Chinese tourists now cruise a road along the Yangtze through the Tiger Leaping Gorge, and luxury lodges dot the cliffs above the Colca Canyon. Our craft has evolved as well. Hot young kayakers with GoPro cameras and Red Bull stickers on their helmets, their lines memorized at every water level and helicopter shuttles at the ready, compete to see who can complete the most runs down the Stikine in a single day.

And yet as I lose myself in water-stained journals in my Blue Ridge office and visit comrades in exploration, from the mountains of Slovakia to the Pacific shores of Venice Beach, to compile these accounts, I find that return is also unnecessary. Those sublime chasms, and the touch of Earth's creation, never left us. Twenty-six years after his seminal exploration of the Grand Canyon of the Colorado in 1869, John Wesley Powell wrote, "[Though it] has been a chapter of disasters and toils . . . [the canyons] tell a story of beauty and grandeur that I hear yet — and shall hear."

Acknowledgments

The greatest joy in creating this book has been the time and recollections shared with so many of my fellow explorers. Some have been known to me for decades on the rivers, others only by reputation as we pursued our parallel river journeys. All were uniformly generous in sharing their time, their dreams, and, in some cases, their demons. The following have my deepest gratitude:

In Europe, Lida Sirotkova and Bernd Kirstein, for introducing me to European slalom and river running in the 1960s and 1970s, and for their essential partnership in researching this volume in the present; Vojtěch Potočý and Čestmír Výtisk, Edith and Michael Memminger, who were so generous with their time, insights, and records; and Jozko Gazda, who shared his personal library of whitewater history,

In Great Britain, Chris Bailey, Dave Manby, Jeff Slater, Chris Bonington, and Paul Presley, editor of *Geographical* magazine.

In Canada, Tony Whittome and Marni Jackson, the wonderfully dedicated mentors behind the Banff Centre's Mountain and Wilderness Writing Residency, who helped this project find its form.

And in the US, Mick Hopkinson, Piotr Chmielinski, Jerzy Majcherczyk, Doug Ammons, Skip Horner, Richard Bangs, Deborah Pratt, Tom McEwan, John Wilcox, Roger Brown, Roger Zbel; whitewater guru Jim Snyder, whose encouragement and introductions have helped guide this book since its inception; Jeff Chapman and his amazing crew at Babelstreet, without whom essential materials in Czech and German would have been unavailable to me; Bob Gedekoh, whose generosity and effort made possible the use of his original painting by Hoyt Reel for the frontispiece, and Chip Fleisher, my incredibly patient editor at Steerforth Press and his amazing team who have made *Torrents* a reality.

Selected References

General

Bartlett, Phil. *The Undiscovered Country: The Reason We Climb*. Ernest Press, 1993.

Coffey, Maria. *Where the Mountain Casts Its Shadow: The Dark Side of Extreme Adventure*. St. Martins Griffin, 2003.

———. *Explorers of the Infinite: The Secret Spiritual Lives of Extreme Athletes — and What They Reveal About Near-Death Experiences, Psychic Communication, and Touching the Beyond*. Jeremy P. Tarcher / Penguin, 2008.

Conefrey, Mick, and Tim Jordan. *Mountain Men: A History of the Remarkable Climbers and Determined Eccentrics Who First Scaled the World's Most Famous Peaks*. Da Capo Press, 2002.

Dugard, Martin. *The Explorers: A Story of Fearless Outcasts, Blundering Geniuses, and Impossible Success*. Simon and Schuster Paperbacks, 2014.

Isserman, Maurice. *Continental Divide: A History of American Mountaineering*. W. W. Norton, 2016.

Long, John, editor. *The Liquid Locomotive: Legendary Whitewater River Stories*. Falcon Publishing, 1999.

Macfarlane, Robert. *Mountains of the Mind: Adventures in Reaching the Summit*. Vintage Books, 2004.

Nichols, Wallace J. *Blue Mind: The Surprising Science That Shows How Being Near, In, On, or Under Water Can Make You Happier, Healthier, More Connected, and Better at What You Do*. Little, Brown, 2014.

Noyce, Wilfrid. *Scholar Mountaineers: Pioneers of Parnassus*. Dennis Dobson, 1950.

———. *The Springs of Adventure*. John Murray, 1958.

Powell, J. W. *The Exploration of the Colorado River and Its Canyons*. Dover Publications, 1961.

Powter, Geoff. *Strange and Dangerous Dreams: The Fine Line Between Adventure and Madness*. Mountaineers Books, 2006.

Roberts, David. *Limits of the Known*. W. W. Norton, 2018.

Williams, Tyler. *Whitewater Classics: Fifty North American Rivers Picked by the Continent's Leading Paddlers*. Funhog Press, 2004.

1. Paradise on the Big Screen: The Indus River

Bangs, Richard, and Christian Kallen. *Rivergods: Exploring the World's Great Wild Rivers*. Sierra Club Books, 1985.

Bowen, Norman R., editor. *Lowell Thomas, The Stranger Everyone Knows*. Doubleday, 1968.

Coles, David. "Searching for Paradise" (illustrated presentation at the Bradford International Film Festival Widescreen Weekend). April 2014.

Keay, John. *The Gilgit Game: The Explorers of the Western Himalayas 1865–95.* Archon Books, 1979.

Lang, Otto. *A Bird of Passage: The Story of My Life.* Sky House Publishers, 1994.

Shipton, Eric. "Nanda Devi." In *Eric Shipton: The Six Mountain-Travel Books.* Mountaineers, 1985.

Thomas, Lowell. *Good Evening Everybody: From Cripple Creek to Samarkand.* William Morrow, 1976.

———. *Search for Paradise* (film), 1957.

Walker, Wickliffe W. *Paddling the Frontier: Guide to Pakistan's Whitewater.* Travel Walji's, 1989.

Webb, Roy. "Search for Shangri-La: The 1956 First Descent of the Indus River by Bus Hatch and a Lowell Thomas Film Crew." *River Runner*, June 1990.

———. *Riverman: The Story of Bus Hatch.* Fretwater Press, 2008.

Yost, John. *Rivers of Surprise / First Descents: In Search of Wild Rivers* (second edition). Menasha Ridge Press, 2010 (reprint from *American Whitewater* May– June 1981).

2. To Get Away from England: The Inn, Colorado, and Blue Nile Rivers

Baillie, Chris. Interview with the author. Aberdeen, Scotland, October 5–6, 2017.

Bonington, Chris. Dispatches to the *Daily Telegraph*, August 16–21, 1969.

———. "Beating the White Water: Five Against the Inn." *Daily Telegraph Magazine*, October 24, 1969.

———. Interview with the author. London, October 3, 2017.

Jones, Mike. Personal records.

Slater, Jeff. Interview with the author. Kelso, UK, October 3–4, 2017.

3. To Dare: The Dudh Kosi River

Bobák, Jiří, and Vladimír Klečka. *V peřejích pod Everestem: Příběh Československých Vodáků* [The Rapids Below Everest]. Olympia, 1978.

Tatra Television. *Forgotten Expeditions.* Televisni Studio Ostrava, 2005. www .czech-TV.cz.

4. Mother of Rivers: The Kali Gandaki River

Hillary, Edmund. *From the Ocean to the Sky.* Viking Press, 1979.

Memminger, Hans. *Kajak Himalaya* (documentary film), 1974.

———. "In den Schluchten des Himalaya." *Kanu-Sport*, April 1975.

———. Personal records.

Piessel, Michel. *The Great Himalayan Passage.* Little, Brown, 1975.

5. A Meteoric Decade: The Dudh Kosi, Orinoco, and Braldu Rivers

Baillie, Chris. Interview with the author. Aberdeen, Scotland, October 5–6, 2017.

Bonington, Chris. *Quest for Adventure.* Hodder and Stoughton, 1981.

Dickinson, Leo. *Dudh Kosi: Relentless River of Everest* (DVD).

———. *Filming the Impossible.* Jonathan Cape, 1982.

Hawkesworth, Chris, executive producer and cameraman. *Colorado: First British Expedition Through the Grand Canyon by Canoe 1971*. Chrisfilm, 1972.

Hopkinson, Mick. "Mike Jones." *White Water Magazine* (UK), November 1978.

Jones, Mike. *The Orinoco*. Mike Jones Films [and Chris Hawkesworth, Chrisfilm], 1978.

———. *Canoeing Down Everest*. Vikas Publishing House, 1979.

———. *The Blue Nile: First Descent of the Blue Nile by Canoe 1972*. Mike Jones Films [and Chris Hawkesworth, Chrisfilm], 1980.

———.. Personal records.

Manby, Dave. *Many Rivers to Run*. Coruh River Press, 1999.

———. Interview with the author. Llangollen, Wales, October 7–8, 2017.

6. Catholicism and Communism in Earth's Grandest Cathedral: The Colca River

Chmieliński, Piotr. Interview with the author. Reston, Virginia, April 1, 2021.

Danielski, Stefan. "In the Shadow of the Falls: Canoandes — 25 Years Later." *Poznaj Świat* [Polish Traveler], March 2005.

Fisher, Richard D. *Earth's Mystical Grand Canyons*. Sunracer Publications, 1995.

Godspeed, Los Polacos! Sourland Studios, 2020.

Goodstein, Carol. "Profile of an Adventurer." *River Runner*, October 1990.

Kane, Joe. "Roaring Through Earth's Deepest Canyon." *National Geographic*, January 1993.

———. *Running the Amazon*. Adventure Library, 1995.

Moag, Jeff. "These Polish Dudes Slipped the Iron Curtain and Changed River-Running Forever." *Adventure Journal*, May 28, 2021.

Piętowski, Andrzej. "Into the Gorge: The First Descent of Colca Canyon." *Explorers Journal*, Summer 2006.

———. *In the Belly of the Earth / First Descents: In Search of Wild Rivers* (first edition). Menasha Ridge Press, 2010.

Polish Expedition Canoandes. *In Kayak Through Peru*. Embajada del Viajero SA, 1984.

Williams, Tyler. "Canoandes." *Canoe & Kayak Magazine*, August 2012.

Wood, Joe. *Funnymen: Life and Times on the Greatest Show on Earth*. Rosedog Press, 2010.

7. The Smoke That Thunders: The Zambezi River

Bangs, Richard. "The Dangerous First Descent of the Zambezi." *Huffington Post*, January 16, 2014.

Bangs, Richard, and Christian Kallen. *Rivergods: Exploring the World's Great Wild Rivers*. Sierra Club Books, 1985.

Lidz, Franz. *Second Descent / First Descents: In Search of Wild Rivers* (second edition). Menasha Ridge Press, 2010.

Wilcox, John, director. *The American Sportsman*, episode 18.1, "Zambezi," ABC TV, aired April 4, 1982.

8. Tiger Leaping: The Yangtze River

Bangs, Richard, and Christian Kallen. *Riding the Dragon's Back: The Race to Raft the Upper Yangtze*. Atheneum, 1989.

Chai Ruikang. "Triumph and Death at Tiger Leaping Gorge." *China Reconstructs*, North American edition 36, no. 4 (April 1987).

Chu Siming. "Rafter's Diary." *China Reconstructs*, North American edition 36, no. 1 (January 1987).

Dickman, Kyle. "The China Syndrome." *Paddler*, January–February 2000.

Fisher, Richard D. *Earth's Mystical Grand Canyons*. Sunracer Publications, 1995.

Li Jing. "Survivor of Rafting Disaster on the Yangtze Says He Still Loves China's Mightiest River." *South China Morning Post*, September 17, 2016.

Liu Qijun. "The Changjiang River Explored," parts 1, 2, and 3. *China Pictorial*, 1987.

Mann, Jim. "American Survives Mountain Ordeal to Get Help for Rafters on Yangtze." *Los Angeles Times*, September 13, 1986.

Maojun Wang. *Diary of the Luoyang Rafting Team*. Web posting.

Nance, Ancil. *1986 Sino-USA Upper Yangtze River Expedition*. Self-published (Ancil Nance, 86 SE Bidwell, Portland, OR 97202), 2014.

Wan Guodong. "Interview with Ken Warren." *China Reconstructs*, North American edition 36, no. 1 (January 1987).

———. "With the Sino-U.S. Yangtze Raft Team." *China Reconstructs*, North American edition 36, no. 1 (January 1987).

Wen Jiao. "The Yangtze Expeditions — A Deeper Meaning." *China Reconstructs*, North American edition 36, no. 4 (April 1987).

Wilcox, John. Interview with the author. Aspen, Colorado, October 1, 2021.

———. producer and director. *Mutual of Omaha's Spirit of Adventure: Rafting and Kayaking China's Yangtze River*, 1986.

Winchester, Simon. *The River at the Center of the World: A Journey Up the Yangtze, and Back in Chinese Time*. Picador, 1996.

Zhe Bian. "Two More Rafting Teams on the Yangtze." *China Sports* 19, no. 3 (1987).

Zheng Guoqing. "Yao Maoshu's Last Challenge: The Changjiang." *China Pictorial*, 1986.

Zheng Hi Lin. "The Long Run." *Explorer, Sports & Tourism Pictorial*, Xizang Province, China, May 1, 1987.

9. The Hardest Thing, in the Purest Style: The Stikine River

Ammons, Doug. *A Short History of the Grand Canyon of the Stikine River*. dougammons.com.

———. *The Laugh of the Water Nymph*. Water Nymph Press, 2005.

———. *Whitewater Philosophy*. Water Nymph Press, 2009.

———. Interview with Jeff McIntyre on InBetweenSwims.com.

Atwood, Margaret. *Strange Things: The Malevolent North in Canadian Literature*. Oxford University Press, 1995.

Gallagher, Nora. *Patagonia: Notes from the Field*. Chronicle Books, 1999.

National Geographic. *Stikine River Fever* (DVD), 2000.

Obsommer, Olaf. *Doug Ammons — Grand Canyon of the Stikine — First Solo Descent 1992* (video). https://youtu.be/8XF7eqEOf_I.

Outdoor Life Network. *Triple Crown of Kayaking*, 1998.

Watters, Ron. *Never Turn Back: The Life of Whitewater Pioneer Walt Blackadar.* Great Rift Press, 1994.

10. As Yet Unknown: The Yarlung Tsangpo River

Baker, Ian. *The Heart of the World: A Journey to the Last Secret Place.* Penguin Press, 2004.

Balf, Todd. *The Last River: The Tragic Race for Shangri-La.* Crown Publishers, 2000.

Boyce, Simon, producer. *Tragedy on the Tsangpo.* National Geographic Television, April 12, 1999.

Cox, Kenneth, editor. *Frank Kingdon Ward's Riddle of the Tsangpo Gorges: Retracing the Epic Journey of 1924–1925 in South-East Tibet.* Garden Art Press, 2001.

Fisher, Richard D. *Earth's Mystical Grand Canyons.* Sunracer Publications, 1995.

Fox, Porter. "Tragedy on the Tsangpo." *Paddler*, March–April 1999.

Gordon, Douglas. "They Don't Come Any Better." *American Whitewater*, September–October 1997.

Heller, Peter. *Hell or High Water: Surviving Tibet's Tsangpo River.* Rodale, 2004.

McEwan, Jamie. *Whitewater to Die for.* AMC Outdoors, March 1998.

———. "Nothing on the Rocks." *Canoe & Kayak*, August 2014.

———. Contemporary audio and written journals.

McEwan, Tom. Interviews with the author. December 14, 1999; June 3, 2002; and June 7, 2002.

———. Contemporary written journal.

McEwan, Tom, and Jamie McEwan. *Trip Report of the Yarlung Tsangpo Expedition October 1998, Lhasa.* November 18, 1998. Limited distribution.

McRae, Michael. "Trouble in Shangri-La." *National Geographic Adventure*, Spring 1999.

———. *The Siege of Shangri-La: The Quest for Tibet's Legendary Hidden Paradise.* Broadway Books, 2002.

Mullen, Kurt. *Unfiltered: Tom McEwan, Athlete, Adventurer, Teacher.* canoekayak .com, September 10, 2010.

Park, Sarah. Interview with the author. December 14, 1999.

Walker, Wickliffe W. *Courting the Diamond Sow: A Whitewater Expedition on Tibet's Forbidden River.* National Geographic, 2000.

Ward, Captain F. Kingdon. *The Riddle of the Tsangpo Gorges.* Edward Arnold, 1926.

ABOUT THE AUTHOR

 Wickliffe "Wick" Walker is a graduate of Dartmouth College, the John F. Kennedy School for Special Warfare, and the Banff Centre for Arts and Creativity. He represented the United States in international whitewater competition at several World Championships and at the 1972 Summer Olympics in Munich. A Fellow of the Explorers Club, he has led whitewater expeditions around the world, including to Bhutan and Tibet. His previous books are *Paddling the Frontier: Guide to Pakistan's Whitewater*, *Courting the Diamond Sow: A Whitewater Expedition on Tibet's Forbidden River*, and *Goat Game: Thirteen Tales from the Afghan Frontier*. He now lives and writes in the Blue Ridge of Virginia.

ABOUT THE ILLUSTRATOR

Kim Abney is a kayaker, caver, explorer, artist, and illustrator. Her previous book illustrations include Phil Coleman's *The Sand Tower* science-fiction series and Doug Ammons's *A Darkness Lit by Heroes* about the 1917 mining disaster in Butte, Montana. She lives in East Tennessee surrounded by horses, cats, and boats.